CW00865167

Time in Head & Heart

by

Kathleen Dyer

authorHOUSE®

AuthorHouse™ UK Ltd.
500 Avebury Boulevard
Central Milton Keynes, MK9 2BE
www.authorhouse.co.uk
Phone: 08001974150

First published by AuthorHouse 9/14/2009

ISBN: 978-1-4343-1714-8 (sc)

Printed in the United States of America
Bloomington, Indiana

This book is printed on acid-free paper.

I dedicate this body of work to both my mothers; Sarah and Patsy; two very beautiful women who are as different as night and day. They have never allowed me to forget my gift from the Creator. They have always encouraged me in words and actions.

To my wonderful sisters of blood and soul, who has always had my back no matter what.

To all the males who have inspired my life. Starting with my father, and my dad, too all my brothers. Not forgetting every friend who has left an indelible mark.

Don't think you are forgotten my very lovely and most talented nieces and nephews, and numerous cousins, aunts and uncles.

To my extended family in New York and here in the United Kingdom, and mostly to my diamond in the rough, and my pillow of exquisite dreams; Montserrat.

For had it not been for you, there would definitely be no me.

Lastly to anyone out there, who thinks that great things never ever happen to dreamers, please do think again. Then take a long and hard look at me Kathleen Dyer; a dreamer in action.

Life is about living, and living well. Believing and doing; if it stirs your heart, by all means go after it. Believe you can do no matter what. The sky is not even the limit 'dude' lovingly reminded m, so endless gratitude to you my dear friend, for always being my other pair of eyes.

I say thank you, thank you, thank you. From the depths of my heart to each and everyone who paved the way so I can be me. You have all done extremely well.

Contents

Birth & Roots

The Gift

God blessed me with a very special and precious gift
Soft and cuddly, and such a bewildering sight to behold
Smelling of sunshine, dewdrop, rain, and a parcel of heavenly
abundance

Already it stirs at the sound of my voice, and clings to my fingers
Touching, and caressing me in places never dreamed of, only
imagined
Blessed with perfection; ten perfect earth-brown fingers and toes
Head covered with a carpet of silky lamb's wool curls that shimmer
like the black sand that kisses up to the curious breaking waves on the
island.
With simmering eyes that shine and burn with such intensity
 Like the brilliance of the sun's rays
Causing my knees to buckle in humility

You chose me?
My God!
You chose me?
At times I can scarce comprehend the meaning of this love and trust
that you placed in me
I am mamma; I will have to be teacher, friend, and at times foe
For you my child at times will not understand why I must say no
I am so overwhelmed
It makes me wonder what on earth I have done to truly deserve
something as faultless and magnificent as you

Inspiration

Where do you find it?
In everything
Opening eyes, feet touching the floor, sounds outside the window
Being alone, with friends, a trip, my next door neighbors, the
argument with mother, sister, brother, friend, lover.
My students, associates, teachers, the teapot, the kettle as it whistles
noisily on the stove
The television, a good book, spoken and written words, color, texture,
crying, laughing, the storm that woke or the one that scared to sleep
Pain, pleasure, anger, hurt, new shoes, old ones
Being lazy, overwork, a great piece of music, a voice, a movie, being
broke, feeling tired
Being still, dancing, writing, reading, playing, making love, feeling
clumsy, singing, walking, looking at leaves falling, listening to water;
rolling, slap, slap, slapping, scampering and slithering through drains,
being poured, or just running at will
Playing in sand, cleaning, cooking, planting, weeding
Taking a shower, dressing, sleeping, shitting, eating, driving, longing,
yearning, creating, buying, selling, whispering, yelling, screaming....
Or just by simply being silent and observing you
Shush!
Please be quiet

Soft yet Loud to Choke the Flow

Loud laughter in head
Accusing eyes
Pointing fingers
Voices; that say you have nothing to say that hasn't been said
Loss of privacy
Failure
Hard-work
Time away from family and friends
Lost moments with a lover
Being shunned
Writers block
Pressure
Not having or finding time
Mother, friend, lover, sister, and brother, even a stranger
Sabotage and undermining
No quiet places, and to much incoming missiles
No faith in your abilities
Blank canvass
The unknown
Just plain and simple fear
Yes FEAR
Fear of success/succeeding
Sensitivity
To self-conscious
Not educating of one self on current events
The past, the present, and most of all the future
To much shit, and definitely to much static

Time Stops

Last fight and hurtful words
A look; poignant and sweet
A touch; feverish and disarming
 A wave
Lipstick on glass, or makeup on collar
Last check written or an unfinished grocery list
The note tucked in the pocket of a favorite suit
The unfinished letter that held more than was ever uttered
The picture falling from book thought forgotten
Hair in a brush or a broken comb
Barrette found, it escaped and lay lodged behind the sink
Smell on clothes that she fears is now fading
The look in her baby's eyes as she stares at him
She is grown now
The sight of her now is seared into memory
You will never be forgotten
Dried flowers, a petal crumbling to the touch
A half-full bottle of your favorite wine
Your optimism
The smile; half-cocked that he gave, you believed it, you trusted it
You placed your heart in his hand
The chip on the side of the chair
The growth spurt marking inside the door way
The heart carved in the back of the headboard
The initials cut out in the trunk of the breadfruit and coconut tree
The oil spot; from the constant banging of your head when we made
love
He is the only one who can make your body moan and cry
She is the only one who knows that special place to tweak, that makes
you howl out of tune
Half- eaten take out because he never made it home
She saw the men dressed in uniform outside, they are seeking out the
house, and they have found it

6

In contemplative mood they walk up the drive
The unexpected delivery; flowers, perfumes some memorable trinket
The child standing at the door looking straight at you
She then finds the courage to ask is she here… this woman who gave
birth to me and gave me away
He has her face; it is drawn with indelible ink
Doctors waiting by bedside, they need to tell you the baby is gone
He gets up to greet the somber surgeon, she didn't make it
The last X made on the calendar
The lipstick curly-q and heart drawn on the mirror
An old movie on the tube
Tears poured forth for the ending of Casablanca
Some funky song we use to sing and dance to
Coming upon a familiar pathway, some road sign you loved to point
out, that made her laugh, him laugh
Remembering your gait
Seeing you running to catch the bus
The way you jumped through the closing train door
The silhouette of you, blinding on another
You turned and the heart stops, then it begins an erratic screaming
Falling snow or the rat-tat-tat of raindrops on galvanize roof
The drip, drip, drip, dripping from drains
She misses you, and God knows she wants you back
He wishes he can call to you, rouse you from where you've gone to
forever lie
Beg you come back, come back to us, come back to me
Have mercy God
Grant ease from this constant aching and yearning.

Dying Young

I looked him in the eyes and he looked into mine
He is falling, time is spiraling
I raced as fast as I could; I had to get to him.
But it seemed as though time and my limbs were against me.

Finally on baited breath I got to him
My mommy, please take me home to my mommy She will make it
better, she will know what to do
Please, please help me get to my mommy.

I shouted and screamed at the top of my lungs
For anyone, someone to please come to our rescue
As I watched, and bore witness to the life essence of this innocent
looking angel seep through my trembling fingers

I cried for the loss of another great doctor, scientist, lawyer, healer...
Over this 'silliness' called bullying; wanting what is not yours, or
simply just because
Just because you think you are bigger, better, tougher
Because you are running with your pack; A 'pack' that can't be honest
enough to say to you, you have done wrong my friend, and what you
did was just not cool
It is not cool to be greedy, selfish, rude, unkind, hateful, lying,
deceiving, and thieving
Being cowardly, hiding out under hoods and caps
Hiding under a river of lies and fancy talk from a system; to afraid of
throwing you and yours off; from becoming and being leeches
As another mother cries, and cradles her dying child's body
As another father calls out for society to bring back corporal
punishment
Better yet give you the right; a life for a life, because she wants you
dead
You who killed her son

You who killed her daughter
You who killed her husband
You who killed her lover
You who killed his father
You who killed his mother, friend, brother, sister
Seeing as spoon feeding and molly-cuddling you hooligans is doing
nothing to aid our society
You in your lofty palaces say, "what good does that do?"
You who haven't lost anyone in such a senseless/stupid way

She walks to his room, and curls up in his bed, and wraps herself in
his blanket
She puts on his shirt
He smells her perfume, and runs his fingers along her comb
She packs away his favorite toys, and reads his favorite book
It never ends, and it doesn't stop
The heart aches and it breaks over and again
Oh God! She needs to breathe
Help Father!
Please help she just needs to sustain the breath, one at a time, from
this wave of sadness that constantly threatens to pull her under

What would you say if you were standing in her shoes?
What would you do if you were sleeping in his bed?
 Listening to these chaotic rhymes and rhythms
They are rumbling around in head and in heart
Especially when she walks torture-some steps to her baby's room
She is reminded that he is no longer there by that sharp kick in her
chest
Oh God she calls as that jagged knife turns and twists in the rotting
regions of her stomach
He is thinking of committing Harry-Carry
Just so you and that corrupt system would get this; that one less
darkie-life doesn't make a better world
Don't think for a second that this puss-filled-and-oozing-out-of-her
mind mother; who is shattered-and twisted, a shell of her former self

will be silencedShe will not be silenced, as you pacify with empty promises.
She wants something done, we want something done
We want it done now. We want it done today
For no other parent should feel or bear this senseless aching over the loss of yet another baby;
A child called 'Hope' and this world's bright future

Something to Think About

M   Members of Parliament

          Mothers

          Ministers in every government

          Mentors

          Me

A   Are you listening?

          Answers for the aching

N   Nothing is being done

S   Shots, stabbing, stealing, slapping, slashing

L   Laughter, for yes we are loosing

A   Angels, assemblymen and women

U   Ugliness, Unfairness

G   Gratuitous, grating on the nerve of good-god-

          fearing people

H   Hurting, hiding, hating

T   Trying; rising after falling

          Trusting; when hearts have been severely wronged and damaged

E   Entrusting a corrupted system with their innocents

R   Releasing and relaxing waiting for an abyss of change

Are You Listening

Wake up! Wake up!
Who me?
Yeah you
You and You
Wake to your brilliance
Leave that little person stunted in growth
Grabbing, snatching, perpetrating, even killing
So you can look like a wannabe
Dressed in tugged-out street wear
Playing at being tough when running with your pack
Bopping and bouncing, gesturing with that arrogant
flair
Canceling words like please and thank you, and
excuse me Sir or Madam
Pushing and shoving
Now happy-slapping and running away laughing
Thinking you the man
Because you made someone feel low-down and oh so damn shameful

Wake up! Wake up!
Who me?
Yeah you
You and You
Wake to your brilliance
Say you are more than a hooded-mumbling-blinged-out-penguin-
shuffling-nuisance
Because a belt that was suppose to have been about the waist is
snuggling up at your knees
How about not being able to tell a girl from a boy; you are lost under
all the layers
Louder than a gonging bell especially when playing your music
through your mobile and daring anyone to say a word about it

But of course the law is on your side.
You 3 years old going on 30
License to do whatever the heck you please out in
the streets and even at home
Even though mom and dad are struggling to keep
food on the table, a roof over your head, and the
latest Nike or Timberland's on your feet
Of course because anything else would just be uncivilized

Wake up! Wake up!
Who me?
Yeah you
You and You
Wake to your brilliance
It is not cool lying to parents about your whereabouts
What you did when you were supposedly visiting friends
Well that is until they ran off leaving you to carry the bag
 An unwanted pregnancy, the gun in a robbery, the purse or wallet of
the victim that fought to the end for his or her life
A husband, wife, mother, child, sister, brother, friend, lover
If only I had known
If only I could see
If only I had someone like you to talk to me, teach me
But all the if-only are now too late

Wake up! Wake up!
Who me?
Yes YOU
YOU, YOU, YOU
Wake to your brilliance
You are better, you are bigger
Think more, say less
Be at your best; do unto others as you would have
done to you
If it doesn't feel right, sound right, seem right, is right
Just say no

Walk away; live/share in another day
Be you, be aware
Wake to you, just you, the best and positive you
Wake to your brilliance
Yes YOU, YOU and of course YOU
SHINE

Pattern/Father Figure

F   Forgiveness, fear, faltering

       Fragrance of the   essence that I am

A   Affecting, avoiding, assaulting, affairs, always

       Such a mass of contradictions in lessons of aloneness, being aware of the next attack

T   Teach, trouble, treachery, tedious, treatment, time, thrills

       Unable to trust in today's promises or tomorrows

H   Hating, haven, home, hands, hitting

       How do we know the next face wouldn't be a reminder of harm?

E   Ecstasy, easy, education, eternal

       A constant cause for editing life

R   Resource, reaching, rating, recycles, redeemable, redemption, reiterate, reminder, remarkable, reptilian

       Running from the roulette of cohabitating

S   Seeing, servicing, speed, smoldering, sperm

       Seeking something profound but just damn scarce in this smorgasbord of 'hue' man; Good ones are scarce, and potentials are locked away in some prison of choice, or gay.

Cuts like a Knife

Looking at her, only through her because you don't see
No words; of thank you, I miss you, no damn I am so happy our
Creator done made you, and leant you to me
No I am sorry for missing birthdays, anniversaries
 No calls just because, not even to ask, "How are you making it today?"
Meanwhile she hears you rushing about asking everyone else

You find the time to ask. "Did you pick up the dry cleaning? Those
two shirts and trousers, did you wash them?"
You should see the way he flits and flutters primp and putter for
Madam whenever she is about
Then pushes and pass by her as though she were yesterday's leftover
There is a catch in his throat when he speaks about a project, down to
the very sports game on television
But only flatness; that is so deafening when he speaks at her, or to
someone about them
Enthusiasm has long since abandoned their ship; their lovemaking is
empty
Fulfillment is a dismal abyss; more torture than pain
Then they lie like bodies in a graveyard
Drunk on regrets, and high on I-told-you-so
Intoxicated on people pleasing, drugged mindless and numb on not
wanting to make an effort
Not now, not yesterday, and probably never

Inspiration & Growth

The Wishes I Dream

I wish a lifetime of happiness for everyone; sons and
daughters, nieces and nephews, friends and lovers
Love understanding and peace
That we would devote more patience and kindness to all those we meet
Acceptance of each other for whom and what we are
Knowledge to want the very best
That we as people would no longer be afraid of each other
That when one hurts we all 'hurt' right back regardless of race or color
That we as a people would make good choices; set examples for the
younger generation to emulate and be proud of
Pride to say I am glad that in the short time allotted, we got to know you
Really knew you from the heart and soul, the CORE
Urgency; to be willing to step in and help, not with violence
Give a thought before mouthing-off; allowing our tongue to spew
what we cannot take back
Commit commitment from friends and lovers
Be true; love, be passionate, make it count in every way
Simple huh?
Now I am counting on you; praying you will help me make them a
reality

Rolling Stone

She has traveled around the world; been to different places, seen
different faces
She has danced with joy and flirted with pain many a time
Her feet have been stuck in shoes to tight; don't feel the pain
To loose; she has left them behind somewhere
The homes; old ones, new ones, clean ones, dirty ones
Sometimes it seems the walls are pressing down and closing in
Never able to fit in, to know just where she belongs
Whose arms are these, hugging, holding, and trying to offer comfort?
The breath caressing, reeking havoc on mind and skin
No rest for tired eyes that wanders; never settling long enough so
other eyes can meet, or connect
Always hoping, always dreaming, looking off to some distant shore
Which direction- the destination; the angle the compass will point
when confusion and mistrust are best-friends
Leaving love and today the here and now to play constant catch-up

Unfinished Blues

Heavy heart burden soul wanting to fly high, fly free
Heart holding a secret
It's tied up, wrapped and bundled, dressed in a pretty package
It smiles, baring cautiousness as its amour, fear as it's weapon
Limbs gnarled branches bare
Blown leaves harvested somewhere
Amidst the blustering howling wind
One loner one solitaire
Gone sunshine gone warm rays
Lingering icy tentacles walking in its wake
No hibiscus morning glory ginger lilies
No bees butterflies no dancing fire flies

Colors of Heart

Legs are tossed wide, exposing blushing pink for eyes to see
As it weeps for the soul pushing its way out
Into a loving and nourishing world of vacuous green and blue
Spoilt by unforgiveness, hatred, misunderstanding, non-
communication, finger pointing, nay saying, doubting and conjuring,
from its inhabitants.
Under a blanket of endless candy floss white and powdery blue; that
says nothing, yet weeps long and hard, grumbling low and loud,
brandishing its wand of crackling electrical pulses to show displeasure
The all-seeing-eye burning yellow furious and fierce; scorching fields
of anything left bare
"I am angry." Mother Nature says.
"And that goes double for Me." snaps Father Time.
They are shaking head, blinking eyes, brandishing fist, and stomping
feet
At a rainbow-meld-and-wonderfully-crafted-bunch of creatures
fashioned by the Almighty
The most skilful hands made Thee
You are crafted like nothing else on the face of this earth
Yet you have no appreciation for the most perfect and priceless gift;
YOU

Me

Eyes that once must have been bright and full of hope
Stare back dull with disappointment and etched with pain
Could that be me one day?
She shivers, as a chill runs through her, up and down her spine,
teasing and caressing like a proficient lover
Her feet appeared glued as she searched your eyes, wondering how
many people actually see you or plan for you.
She wonders, how do you feel today on this blistering cold day, other
than damn cold?
What are in your nightmares, do you even dream?
Where is home?
Is it under a bridge, in a car, in a run down building or a back alley?
Where stray animals are your neighbors, and bullets and engines
back-fire in loud crescendos
Where the wind howls in fits of anguished wails, as rain beats and
pelts like soaked leather upon tired stretched and aching skin
Where excited and often times sickening moans of ecstasy are your
strains of hip hop, bee box, or rhythm and blues…
Newspapers, empty cartoons and crates of anything tossed aside from
passer by's are your bouquets, and Graffiti; expressive and downright
jarring are your murals
A gun stuck in your amigos face while he is on his knees begging for a
much loved life; pounded and painted with broad strokes of adversity
that is now left to rot, becoming compost for things to grow, only to
be leveled, or by chance it is stumbled upon
Now most cast down eyes and turn up nose, you are only an after
thought
Beggar or drifter they surmise, must have done something to deserve it
You are forgotten; pushed aside for yet another new and sparkly story
Discrimination, bad luck or hard times, misfortune and bad spending…
"Shit! I have no boundaries." Homelessness says. "For today him,
tomorrow it could be you.
I am coming for YOU."

Notes

Often heard it said that we in de last days
Last days? What do you mean?
I use to wonder what on earth mamma was talking about
Until she said, "Look!"
 Look around you child
I looked, and looked but nothing seemed different, just a bit out of
sorts
Silly girl look deeper, look deeper and longer at all de out of sorts

Now I see! Yes mama now I see!
Cause a volcano that been sleeping foo years now wake up and start
spewing out its belly; rocks and dust for miles and miles
It send peaceful and conniving folks running; scattering them
through all walks of life
Leaving de place ripe for all kinds of conniving
They bombarding we Paradise with ton-load a drugs and guns, we
even got prevalent prostitution; shipping in coolie replacing darkie,
you could get it anywhere you turn pan we island
Everyone wants to compete with de Joneses and buy and sell like
Donald Trump
Some want to be tugged out like Snoop Dog and pony bouncing like
Beyonce

Corruption reaching new heights to de point where they shooting-up
and picking off each other like dying petals falling from tired roses
No respect foo each other, none for their elders, and none for the
innocent, and certainly none foo themselves
Children getting molested, women raped, beaten, and killed, and
their bodies thrown away like waste, carcass bare like yesterday's
garbage bin
No peace in de Middle East, they still fighting and warring like
Can't even say like cat and dog, because animals now learn to get
along

Can't even go out foo de evening anymore cause instead of using
common sense to solve arguments, people relying on guns and knives
Well foo argument sake some say guns don't kill, it is de people who
use gun to kill each other
But yet we don't give a shit
He hear nough noise and huffs out to go talk, or beg them stop
making noise so he child could sleep, and he never come back
Take de Oklahoma bomber who killed all those people
They found him guilty! Yes they did
But yet he still get de right to fight for a 'right' he willfully stole from
others
So tell me what nerve
He got heart like breadfruit eh?
Now come them fools going by de name of de Trench Coat Mafias;
having so much more than de average family who work from dust till
dawn, yet still don't bring home half of what those spoilt brats pay for
their guns, and materials for their bombs
All under de so-call watchful eyes of parents
Jus wondering how hard them parents was looking
These parents who 'tend' their children like prince and princesses; to
afraid to tell them they are rotten and rude, and another mouth off is
going to see them swallowing what teeth they have
Better yet march to take back the right to raise your child, other than
leaving them to be reared by the government; that tells children they
have rights especially if parents talk a certain way, or lift their hand to
them when they give grieve
I ain't forgetting you the parents who let the television rear your
children because you can't be bothered
Or those who are like needles in a haystack; gallivanting about trying
to insinuate themselves into the next best thing
Parents we are our children's keepers, we should not spare the rod and
spoil the child
Can't you see that we nearing de end if we allow these ferile children
to reek havoc on society

People let us help ourselves and this world
Help de world to cleanse itself and let it begin with us; you and me

Just look and see, feel
It is summer and yet it feel like winter, sun still up when moon
should be flirting
Flowers and trees get fool; thinking its time to put out leaves, and
sprout flowers
Fourteen year old girls are having babies
Suicide and genocide
How about normal children having plastic surgery, parents trying to
further perfection; a flat nose to be straighter, like they sniffing out
shit when they look at you
Implants in breasts that are still not fully developed
Then they wander about wringing hands and wondering how they
gonna pay the mortgage on an already overpriced house, or a run
down apartment
Where is de honor in husbands betraying wives to sleep with their
daughters, and women with their sons?
How about employers who think they can overwork and underpay?
Expecting to still get 150% and then some outta you
Then there are de doctors who sit and think they are like de Creator
when they brag and boast about cloning
Telling us they have only cloned sheep
Yeah right
Think they ain't got a human on de freezer somewhere
After all they have simulated kidneys, lungs, grafted fingers, hands
and only God-knows-what-else
They give men vaginas, and women balls
Then why not take it a step further; how about making men give
birth; feel all de pain and suffering we as women go through
Can I get an Amen?
Before it was Ecstasy, Ginseng, Flash and Speed, Now what do we
have?
Yeah, we got Viagra with a promise of more sexual potency, and God
forbid the condom buss
No worries man!
 You gat de Morning After pill
Not that it is a bad thing, because it good to know a woman got a
choice for just-in-case

Sex, sex, sex
 It no longer taboo
You turn on de idiot box and it there foo all to see
But they only seem to be enhancing it more for men; who on top you pounding away lek they digging a ditch
Then they have de blasted nerve to ask, "you feel me baby?"
"Yes baby! Yes baby! She screaming
Meanwhile she lying there thinking bout all de things she got to do, that he ain't gonna help with
He tired, trying to clear de goldmine, can't handle it, so he roll over, and fall fast asleep, snoring like a sickly beached whale

Hear bout de special chip they gonna implant in de babies?
And speaking of babies, hear you can chose de specific sex you want?
What about those countries where a certain sex get murdered because to have them around would weaken de society
What a laugh huh?
When we cocksure it got more men pan them lazy ass than women
And what are they doing?
Sing it sistah!
Playing video games, and watching de Cyclops.
They got to catch up on their football and basketball game
Becoming irate and more cantankerous, and ever so blasted 'mean'
Hey!
Hear you can now go baby shopping instead of grocery shopping?
Parents selling their babies to de highest bidder
Got ¼ of a million?
Well regardless if you a pedophile or a mass murderer buy ma baby
So I can wear Gucci, Tommy, Moschino and Manolo Blahnik, or some overpriced Jimmy Chou
Stuff that can feed a tiny nation when calculated
But they don't seem to care-a-damn
Not even for those struggling with poverty and hunger running rampant in their own backyard
Neither a care for Africa; Sudan, Darfor, Rwanda, and Mogadishu

Then again where is de honor when another human can refer to his or her skin-color brother and sister to a cockroach, and litter the road with their bodies like asphalt
Some are drinking from golden goblets, and tossing meat to dogs that can feed many villages
Chopping off limbs and holding them high like trophies as they grin from ear to ear, dancing like they are possessed
How about raping innocent babies thinking it can cure AIDS
How in de hell do you sleep, and play with your children after an act so downright heinous?
What if it was done to yours?
When and how do we stop these monstrosities from continuing?
Have mercy heavenly father, please have mercy

How about showing up and blowing people up, strapping a bomb to yourself and not being afraid to set it off, thinking you will be hugely rewarded by Allah
Violence and more violence, have you forgotten the commandment; thou shalt not kill
The entire world just seems so satiated, like we developing a special sickening immunity to all de atrocities
So we crave more and more
Then when the reality of the thing comes home to roost
Lord have mercy!
We then hang heads and bawl long water from we eye saying we never expected it
Bullshit!
Like for instance shooting an unarmed man forty two times and getting off with a mere slap to the wrist
Because you who wear a uniform, and carry a license; A license to you which means a person of color can be dictated to by a lying, cheating, and undercover-racist with no family values
 An immoral-prick so poisonous, reeking, insidious, corrupt to the very core
Yet he is 'keeper' of the law

A ten year old singing about adult copulation and referring to a girl or a woman as a BITCH

You weren't brought into this world by a BASTARD were you little boy; who gets rewarded in millions to buy cars he's not even to the legal age to drive

Not to mention the 'bling-bling' that has a life of its own, so much so he seems to be falling under the weight

Defacing and desecrating a person's final resting place.

I beg you people stop the madness before we all end up in a hell of our own making

Stifled and strangled by all of those things we have closed our minds, hearts and yes our eyes to.

Eyes

Friendly, striking, blazing, blinding eyes
Eyes in people who smile yet hate
Laughing, crying, judging, pitying eyes in you
She can't believe it!
They were only waiting
Glad, questioning, informing, betraying eyes
The first to say, "Should have happened to you a long time ago
Hopeful, wishing, loving, thankful eyes that couldn't wait to welcome
you
Trusting, believing, calm, bright eyes that asks are you happy to see
me?
Confused, plotting, cold, dying eyes asking do you mean me harm?
Deceitful, searching, sparkling, prying eyes that know you see, you
believe, you forgive
A look can speak with volumes
Causing major break down in homes and lives
Start wars, bring on guilty verdicts, keep you trapped and tied in
knots
They can 'wound' just like weapons
These eyes, your eyes, are the best and worst of us

Monotony

Jumper on the roof
Victim swan diving from a bridge into murky water
House wife and new mother ups and pops a bottle of pills chasing it
with vodka
Little Ben, Pretty Mary, can't talk to mommy
Tif 'ny and Lasandrea; they have no idea who daddy is
Meet Father D fondling children, while Pastor Pete is screwing
around with Mr. and Mrs. Jones
Down low they calling it, meanwhile bishop and priests manhandling
their dick
While Sister Martha dress up like Madam Des'ree and walk atop their
backs in spike heels, and whip their ass to a rosy blushing pink
Oops! Did I say that?
She is tired of being his punching bag and slave
The go-to-girl always with her plastic smile, and bending like a
pretzel to everyone's beck and call
They pass you over and over for that damn promotion
Even knowing you can do the friggin job with your eyes closed
After all haven't you been carrying the lazy-ass-limp-dick-two-minute.
Still your tongue girl
How about Lady Liberty who must always jet off to the water cooler
when Mr. Wonderful, packing bulging shoulders and zipper, stops by
to deliver mail
He doesn't even know she exists
How many times are you gonna drive that blasted vehicle up and
down, and round about, those crowded streets as a bus driver?
Watching pushy, bored, noisy housewives and slutty and half-naked
unintelligent and loud girls and vacuous pimply-faced boys and lazy
ass men
He is thinking, she is thinking, want to spread her, want to push him
atop the wheel and lay her/him out with some serious f******
Shit!

Can't believe it, fast forward; they are so out of your league,
unattainable, some cause a bitter taste or bile to burn in stomach
It doesn't sink in no matter how many times you've explained at
nauseam to that snot-nosed brat; who spits and curses
Society says no more corporal punishment
No touching to show care or concern
Nowadays affection spells like trouble that carries a stiff penalty
So you watch little cherub-face Billy turn into a bullying bigoted
crime-committing-jail-hopper
Prayers are taken out of the schools and omitted from homes
Everyone wants to be to 'god-damn politically correct'
Reach for your pocket book and hold it tight, walking down the
street, as you come upon a gaggle of youths especially if they are
wearing hoodies
Oh! Oh!
I am a black man
D W B means you will be pulled over and questioned constantly by
silly uneducated police officers
Especially if they come upon you in an affluent neighborhood, or
behind the wheel of a fancy car
Selling your body for a greedy bastard who takes most of the money
and pumps you full of drugs, beat and oftentimes have his way then
discard you like yesterday's newspaper
Bling-bling and fancy threads are more important than food or a roof
over your head
How she is asking, and why he is wondering
Sunday to Saturday, January to December
Up and down and in and out
Young and old; once a man twice a child
Seasons come and seasons go
It goes bad and gets horribly worst for long periods
Days shorter and money scarcer,
Caring; love in its simplest form shows up rare and more rare
More giving than receiving, and less and less understanding
Mother Nature is becoming as bitchy as a cranky spinster
Summer days feel like fall
Flowers budding before their due time

Trees dying faster than you can blink an eye
Forget Father Time; he is a typical male; over before you can say
touch me here, feel me there
Sun rise its time to set
No wonder babies no longer maturate they mutate
No creeping, just up and strolling
No more milk mommy I want Mc Donald's
Aren't those Timberland's just 'WICKED' daddy

To Much to Soon

Oh God not yet
 It is definitely to soon
Stop, stop, stop, I beg you please stop
Slow down, please slow down
I have only just opened my eyes
Thoughts running here, bouncing off of there
Can't grab a hold of one before the other pounces in
The telephone is ringing, ringing, ringing
Questions upon questions
All these continuous incessant questions
Slow down please down
I've only just opened my eyes
Snap, Snap, Snap
I am going back to bed, gonna close my eyes
I am closing you out
The head-aching questions, noises, puzzle-solving,
Reasoning why must you?
How come she?
Is he going to call?
I am hornier than a toad, but if I tell you this what?
What would you think?
Are you going to call again?
How long before you disappear?
Are you safe?
What else is going to happen today?
The job, hours, money, friends
Why are people so uncaring of each others feelings?
What am I going to do so I don't end up bored out of my skull?
The children, the in-laws, the girlfriend, the boyfriend, the lover
Slow down, slow down

I am awake
I am listening
I am wanting
I am hoping
I am believing
So you see you haven't won yet

Looking Forward To Spring

Didn't think this was possible
But alas!
She is slowly coming out of the dark
Don't get it twisted though
For she still wishes with all her heart that it would be you on the
other end of the telephone every time it rings
Disrupting her I will get over you, I know I will song
I'll pretend my heart is not broken
But heck! Hold up!
It is broken you bastard! You broke her heart
She gave you the hammer to smash it to hell
Pound it to smithereens
Especially on those days when all she wanted was to stay in bed with
the covers pulled up over her head, and not be bothered with the
outside world
But like plants and trees have wick, so does the heart
For it is looking forward to spring

Spring Is Coming
She has paused and looked up
She has even smelt the roses, and accepted a compliment
She's once again believe that she is beautiful
She's said thank you" when one of your namesake opened up a door
for her
Smiling that bullshit boyish come hitter grin
"Excuse me miss, what's your name, where are you from?
"No! No! No!" She could hear her strangled voice screaming.
I have been there and done that, so not today mate, but someday
Yeah someday she's gonna rise up singing, and will probably never
want to wring your bloody neck, or yank your lying lips from your
tormenting face, with those deceiving eyes
Yes Spring is definitely coming
Her heart has got wick, it is ready to bloom once again

So she will not be writing you letters, or composing sappy poems like the one she sent you a couple of weeks ago
No she will kinda-sorta forget your face
She will close her ears and hurting heart to your deceptive words
She will get that 'pep' back into her step, that rhythm in her heart
She will once again feel in all the places above her waist, and yes dear God even below
She will rise like a phoenix from the ashes, when her best friend will not have to rouse her, or talk her soothingly to sleep
Yes Spring is coming
Spring is coming
Spring is coming
Hello she heard her say to a fellah, my name is....
Yes! Spring is finally here
She is alive and ready to battle for her life.

Remember Remember
That Day in September

9/11/2001

Trade Center Bombing

Prayer from a Worrier

Dear God it is only me your worrier
Just alarmed at the chaos that has crippled my adoptive place of
residence
Why couldn't you tell us?
Why didn't you give us a sign?
That is the cry on every lip
Where were you when this insidious act was put in motion?
When these plans were finally carried out?
Did you not show yourself?
Give those cowards a cold stare?
Tell them you will hold them personally responsible for all the lives
they were threatening
Now stolen in trust, time, lending a helping hand, visiting, working
My God!
Why?
Where were you?
Where was your sister friend Mother Nature?
Your bosom buddy Father Time
Couldn't you both have shifted things?
Blown a sweet soft kiss, set things on a different course
However in retrospect, where else would have made it better?
Oh my God!
This is just so much, too much
Remember this coverage from the 40's; where people had to learn the
'crouch and cover'.
Preparing oneself for impending doom; the chance you might be
caught when the big one hits
Doom's Day; shaking up everyone's existence
Now we know what they were feeling, because we are feeling it now
That false sense of security, especially when we saw our massive
structures crumble like communications between feuding nations
Now battles are raging red-hot
Over a look, down to a touch; a brush-up against

Even down to the clothes you wear
People are feeling betrayed and abused
They are feeling as though they were taken advantage of; bamboozled
because their guard was lowered for an instant
Now words are weapons, having the power to evoke such horrible
pain and tragedy
So Father-God why?
Why did you give the breath of life; allowing these fanatics to enter
this realm, to cause such immense chaos
When you knew each of us even before we were an inception
Pro-life and choice
All this we know in the intellectual scheme of things
But watching the willfulness of this wretched act
Of a mother, father, sister, brother, friend, lover
Not having the chance of ever again receiving a hug, or kind word of
encouragement
The one bright spark, the caretaker and motivator
That second source that infuses the will inside you to go on
Gone is that treasure who can't share in another smile, dance…
He is gone
She is gone.
Now my question to you is why
Why are those responsible for this very cowardly and senseless act still
breathing the precious gift of life?

Chaos

God it is coming!
Oh my God!
Oh my God!
Didn't you see the first one?
Oh my God!
Oh my God!
Look at the other one
 It is heading straight for them again!
It hit it! It hit it! It went straight for it!
So precise; it was as if the action was meticulously calculated from
every angle
Bellowing puffs of smoke curled and shouted to the heaven
Ferocious ash and metal crumbled, falling, falling, raining, and
rushing down on the chaos below
As orange, amber, and red like shiny jewels, squealed and wheezed
Decorating people like blankets of flowers in springtime
Allowing tons of toxic gasoline to sprits' the air like pricey perfume,
asphyxiating every sense
Hands are reaching out and feet are clawing and scrambling
Limbs are being looked at in dazed-amusement, while some are
reckoning; should they be collected
Eyes are blinded, some forcibly squeezed shut, it is too much to
decipher
The stomach lurches and spits
"I will not leave you...I promise."
"Help me, please help me, help me please."
"What is happening? I just went to get coffee."
"I tried to call my wife."
"Get away from me! Get away from me!"
"Don't leave me… Please… Please don't leave me."
"Go! Go save yourself."
"Tell my husband, my Amy, Maggie, Willy, my..."
We had a terrible fight; I can't even remember what it was about."

"This is my family." He said clutching the picture. "I was going to become a permanent resident soon. I got my call from immigration. "
"I can't find Lucy. I can't find my Louise. "
A mom rushed to the television and screamed and hallowed
A father howled and bawled, breath sucked in and was held, it burned to much expel it
Her son, daughter, friend, lover, neighbor
They are there...No...On there way there
Please keep him safe God let him be safe, bring him home, he isn't a good man, he is as mean as a fierce cold wind, but he is all we have
"Mommy is Katie okay? When is she coming home?"
"Soon baby. Soon you'll see." She said with a prayer on her lips, as she held the telephone hard and close against her ears.
But all that offered comfort was the incessant ringing, then it suddenly all went SILENT
Slow, slicing, segregating, with silence so sickening
Illusions shattered, it intoxicated many
Loneliness stretched on like a bottomless pit
Everlasting and eternal
Noxious and nasty
Tedious, trailing, teasing and threatening
The silence was so damn deafening
It challenged, it crushed, it weakened
It disrupted civility, it haunted mind and body
Her knees buckled, he crumbled in a heap
Suddenly we knew, they knew without a doubt
That the entire world would change; nothing would ever, ever, ever be the same again

Death

Death is peeping
Death is crawling
Death is circling
Death is searching
Death is coming
Death is smiling and smelling
Death is tangible, death is here

Look at what they've thought up
Look at what they've brought to my doorstep
This is what they have done

Death is crying
Death is weeping
Death is staring
Death is reeking
Death is cradling and moaning
Death is confused

Death says, "You are in my embrace, close your eyes now and go to
sleep."
You are safe
You are safe
You are safe now
Death writhes
Death moans
Death wails
Death weeps
Death is still weeping

??Dying??

Bright lights
A kaleidoscope of colors
Bursting energy
Bouncing images
Stinging and jarring
Oftentimes melodious and so still and peaceful
Questioning and wanting
Wishing and praying
There is so much still to say
Regrets and hurting
A death to repay an apology
Not now, oh God not now, I am not ready
Give me one last chance, I will give you anything
Please… Please…Please…
Yes
Finally sweet release
Eternal rest
Is it?

Coming Out Of the Dust

There is chattering and laughing
A sense once again of coming out from under the rubble
Mind you no pun intended
For these are trying times we are living in
But through it all there is a glimpse of hope again
Brothers and sisters have begun to go about without that forlorn look
registered on their faces.
The sky is coming alive; Planes are flying, it looks more blue than
grey
People are not walking anymore looking up
Before it was the odd one or two every couple of hours, now more
frequent
Even the heaven doesn't seem so sad, it has stopped pouring buckets
Someone said, "The heaven is weeping. Our Creator is sad. "
Stripes and stars are flying from roofs vehicles and buildings
Yellow ribbons are tied around trees
Statements are being made
Promises are being kept
As if to say '**yes we have been wounded but we shall not give up
totally. We are down but we will not let you; you who tried to take
our way of life
away prosper. We will not give you the last laugh, the final say.**
You group of 'animals' parading your tyranny in the name of justice
You who tried to change the face of our nation
Not just America
You may know someone; who knows someone
The cycle continues
Good or bad, right or wrong
You claim you fight in the name of Allah
But isn't Allah for peace?
Tell me what is going on here my brother, my sister
You pray to Allah, we pray to God
Enlighten me, what is the difference?

Here are the best bits though
Laughter; the laughter of the children
The scolding voice of a parent
The lilt that colors a piece of gossip; that has nothing at all to do with
the dreaded words; Nine Eleven or Trade Centre Bombings
Where you were so afraid to turn the television on because of the
repetitiveness of all the stations
To the point where it is memorized; programmed deep into your
subconscious
You eat, breath, sleep and speak of the cursed tragedy
You are immune to it, so desensitized; you no longer flinch or cower
Even though you keep expecting the next shoe to fall
Because someone said, bad things come in three's
We have begun to get back to the task of what's at hand
Living; Breathing, grieving, dusting off, burying, loving, and
rebuilding

P.S
Never forget to say I love you to just that one person in you life who
means the world to you
Little steps; hugging, encouraging laughter, a kind word, a good deed
Because like September 11th 2001 proves
Your world can come crashing down about you
Changing things drastically in the blink of an eye

Have Mercy

We pray for forgiveness in huge chunks
So as not to buy into the crazy hype floating about
Enabling and feeding the hurt and hating in a name
Some call you Allah, others say God
Some respond by saying Jah Rastafari
But to whomever all the cries and calls are uttered
When we fall on knees and hands, placing face and lips to the
ground, casting troubled and tearful eyes upward
Please forgive, grant ease to a chaotic and brooding world
Tossed into peels of upheaval
Everyone is slipping and sliding in the muck and mire of the dodging
of questions
Or answers come in the form of bullets and missiles, and senseless
killings
Have mercy!
Have Mercy!
Have Mercy!
Is the prayer now on so many shivering lips

Our Prayer

I pray you hear our prayer, and answer when we call
Even though we may be cruel, when others are unkind
Let this be our prayer, and embrace us when we fall
Keep us in your care, and hold us in your love
Lead us Lord, and keep us safe

This body is so weak, the spirit is failing fast
They say, child just be strong, but Lord just for how long
Patience my child, it's already done, bought and paid for, it will be
alright

She prays for strength, to keep holding on
But Lord you understand, that I am just a man
So keep mind strong, and pressing on
Sometimes this vessel tends to be unworthy, straying fast and further
Lord from you
But you understand that we are only human, and making mistakes is
so common in everything we do
Hurting, stealing, corrupting, propagating
Day after day, each second of the day
How long will your spirit strive, forgiving ten times ten
But Lord you are on our side, no matter that we are wrong
Walking with us and keeping us strong
We feel your presence near
We give to you our hands
For you to guide us always on
Guide us to your grace, guide us to you place
To a place where we will all be safe/free

These words came from constantly listening to the song; The Prayer sang by so many Andre Bocelli, Celine Dion, Yolanda Adams and Josh Groban
I found the strength to always be positive in the face of so many disappointment and trials since September 11th 2001.

Pride and Strength

Essence of my Island

Atop a rocky precipice carpeted in fields of green; jade, mint, hunter,
sea-foam, spruce and forest
Under the azure canopy of dawn's early light
Overlooking aqua and navy, mixed with cobalt, to give it that
powdery flair
Blanketed by a carpet of clay; burnt brown, and sienna, glistening like
topaz under the glare of a hot sun
Black speckled with flecks of coral beige
Inhaling fresh mouthfuls of salty sap-laden, earthy, fruit filled, visceral
flora and fauna
Tasting juices in gulps of tangy passion fruit, tart citrus; lemonade,
tamarind and swivel-sweet
Creamy mouthfuls that slide down the back of your throat in the
form of sour sop, mango and lick-kissing guava nectar
Biting into the succulent flesh of mouth watering fried chicken, and
hand-kissed-by-God rubbed fish and meat
Swallowing spoonfuls of richly spiced stews, and soups; goat water,
red bean, black eye, pumpkin, and pigeon peas
As myriads of colorful clothes and head wraps, trickle by, upon the
rainbow collection of faces
As they lounge, or in walking, playing, riding, running and dancing

Island Rhapsody

Woke with a start and listening keenly
Heart thumped, thumped, and thumped in chest, as ears peeked
Not accustomed anymore to the wind playing hide and seek, and singing
She had forgotten how it would whip about the island, helter-skelter
Rapping tenderly, then creeping under floor, and rubbing against
windows and doors
"Come out, come out." It seemed to call.
 "It's time to get up and move about."
She looked over at the clock, it winked back that it was only 5:30am
It was her first time visiting on the island after 17 years of being
absent, and man had things change!
But actually to the trained eye most things had remained the same

"Come out, come out." The wind called again. From closer; inside
the room, bringing her up and out of bed.
No doubt having climbed up the wall, and crawled through window.
"Okay, okay." She tossed
Jumping out from among sweaty covers, to the imp that had found
its way inside to harass and tempt her.
"Rise and shine girl of kindness, ability, talent, honesty and heart,
loving, ethereal, earnest, never-ending"
She loved being awakened by that beat; sultry and oh so sweet.
Like the first strains of the masquerade drums or Jump-Up music
come the beginning of 'Festival Season'.
Now the roosters joined in
"You are full of personality and very progressive,
earthy, always able, reasoning and reaching, loyal and learning,
interesting, new and enchanting."
"Tell me more, sing me more." She begged.

She sought out abandoned-at-the-end-of-a-long-day slippers, and
pushed her feet into them, and reached for her robe, and hurried into it
She tiptoed to the living room, and reached for the door handle.

"Come join us my friend; who is deep, yearning, effective, and a most righteous lady.
Lady of the island, daughter to our Montserrat, and soul-sistah-friend too many
We sure did miss you.
So come let us welcome you officially.
Look! See all who we brought out to wish you well.
The wind kissed at her face a couple times, it tickled her eyes, fussed up hair, and boldly crawled up shirt and trouser legs
It made every part of her being stand to attention
She wished her other half had made the journey
However he had respected her need to do this on her own.
Her eyes sort out ten roosters, strutting about, they stopped suddenly to look up at her curiously
Where was that blasted camera she cursed, having vowed never to put the thing down?
For no one would believe this incredible sight, even if she told it a hundred times over
For she was being worshiped and adored in all her funky-breath and-sleep-twisted-glory
Fingers-on-a-hand lizards, dressed in green and beige, fussed with flitting birds; who tried to seat themselves atop green coconuts on the midget tree
Three meowing cats, and the yard dogs; Norman and Bruce, along with a couple others howled.
"You are all so beautiful." She muttered, as tears streamed down her face
She felt them when her hands meandered up to her cheeks.
Eyes sought the sky to murmur a thank you to the heaven
Even that seemed so close, that all she had to do was reach out and touch the beauty; huge white and grey puffy clouds standing still for a blink of an eye, then off they bobbed
She smiled and tore her eyes away to wander down to the blanket of cobalt blue for endless miles
She heard the distant waves break at the shore.

The bells begun to peel heralding a joyous welcome
Common sense told her though they have been ringing in 6:00 am across the island for years.

So worshipers can gather, and the working sect can now begin to stir, it was a reminder that it was another brand new day

A brand new day, first of many for two weeks here on the island of her birth

Footsteps crept in on her reverie

It came from a donkey that housed an elderly man

He sung and hummed a familiar tune, and try as she may she couldn't recall it

They were making their way up the well worn asphalt

"Marning Miss! Enjoying de day de Lord done bless us wid?"

"Yes Sir." She called back to him; barefooted and raggedly dressed; from his weather beaten hat, to his dry ashy feet.

But he looked tremendously contented, as he smiled; showing a huge gap and what looked like fangs clawing dreadfully unto his huge gums

"Gonna go hoe up some pitear'ta/potato, I go bring you back a couple. You like?"

"Thank you Sir."

"Call me Mas Edwin man. No need for formalities. I neva seen you roun these ya-parts before. Visitin?"

"Yes Sir. I mean Mas Edwin. I am visiting from England for two weeks."

"Well enjoy you self. I will come by wid de pitear'ta late'tah/later."

"Ok." She said. "Thank you very much."

He waved her off, and continued on his merry way

She waited until he passed to go on with her perusing.

Sniff…Sniff

The smell of smoke; a burning coal pit mingled with the dampness and vegetation, stirred with the salt air

That is until the sweet aroma of coffee assaulted her being

A cup was placed in her hand

Oh God

She sipped and sipped again

Welcome home her host said again, let the magic bathe you, seep through you, one breath at a time.

She was transported to Paradise here on earth

She had forgotten that Heaven was right here on Montserrat lovingly known by many as The Emerald Isle of the Caribbean

Her Majesty/La Soufriere

She demanded a meeting face to face
Yet she never said when, so we were left to choose
So we pushed our way picking through the rain and wind, bumps,
and twists and turns, up to see her Her Majesty stood stalwartly
awaiting our presence, decked out in her splendiferous array; a
flowing ball gown of verdant green to the left, and burnt to the crisp
ash to the right.
Her jewellery; was an eclectic blend of old and new crevices and
fissures molded and crafted in ash
Grey puffy clouds crowned her, while breezes blew off the sea and
surrounding mountains to fan her
She said nor offered anything/nothing
Yet we felt her presence letting us know that at anytime she could
crush us alive with just a cough or sneeze.
Her guards; huge boulders and mounds of earth stood like
centurions, and mastiffs at her feet
"Well go on, she urged, get your ooh's and aah's out, click your
zealous photographs whether I want you to or not
Make your money; in songs, stories and poetry
Come with your busses, and truck tours, your packed cars and vans
Come by sea and air, point and curse, rant and rave
Flail your arms as you sit in judgment, in your so call protected
towers and observe me."
We thought her boastful and braggy
Of course we didn't dare say that as we cowered like suck-ups beneath
her
"Look at me, worship me. I know how much you fear me, standing
there groveling, when with one belch from my sulphuric belly I could
lay you as fodder to the wind
Don't think for a second that I do not see and hear all
For every one of these cracks and veins keeps me plugged into the
heart of everything

I am Her Royal Highness/Queen of The Soufriere Hill. Yes you heard me. That is who I say I am. And don't you dare look away. You had better love me, worship me and fear me. For as much as I took away I gave back

Look at the masses I brought flocking to your shore

For so many had not known about you Montserrat and your people.

Now you are the toast on every lip

I divided and conquered, I brought all to their knees

From rich to poor, captain to crook

I kept you busy in the day, and so very restless at night; haunting your minds and hearts.

I put the fear of the Holy Ghost like a phobia to some about you.

I hypnotized; there is a spell on you, the more you criticized and flee, the more you ran back to me and so do the many others you have touched

As much as I am a nuisance in my ruling; with heavy fist, you stick to me like flies to shit

I am a part of you, as you are in me

You love me, and I love you right back

I put a spell on you

I am your Royal Highness/Your Majesty/Lady Soufriere

Hugo the the Uninvited Guess

Who is this thing who wants to come for a visit?
Yearning to pass through a we lovely Emerald Isle
So disrespectful
Hear it bringing along 150 miles per hour gale force wind and
torrential rain as companions
But we Montserratian's; a beautiful and colorful, good natured, hard-
working, simplistic, creative tillers-of-the-soil, stirrers-of-tasty-pots;
goat water and Pelau
Cantankerous! Especially if you frig-dem-up; letting you sheep run
wild to eat up them flowers bush and grass
How about stoning them tamarind, and picking they mango and
limes without permission
How about always begging foo you healthy breadfruit, especially
when you been eying it foo de longest-ah-time
Not forgetting Sarah passing wid she nose up in de air, wid she people
dem from foreign, pretending she don't see you
Or Tyrell de fisherman passing he best catch over you head
How about them rude picknee; always pushing they motor-tire wheel
cross you fresh swept yard
Now all that coming to a halt because everyone need help boarding
up them windows and ting
Lord it so funny to see Miss Patsy lovely picture window with a big
slab of plywood press up against it
How about Annie always bragging bout she mansion that everyone
calling a ranch, cause she got she foolie-man every minute adding on
yet another wing
Mas Pete can't visit Tante!
 She husband home a keep de roost hot , hot, hot

Well Hugo coming is de cry on everyone's lips
No turning back now, nothing anyone can do
So de island become a ghost town set foo a showdown, after a couple
of hours of running round trying to stock up pan food, water, and
more lumber

It flying up about de place faster than an urban development in the United States
Hugo is on its way the oppressing dry heat and humidity shouted
Along wid de ever rapid and growing moroseness of de sky
So anxious people start saying their good-art-noon and goodnight
Crawling in and awaiting this unwanted-yet-nothing-you-can-do-about-it comp'ny

Then late evening you begin to hear pit-pat that turn into bop-bap
Distant rumbling come a knocking, then start up an unholy raucous with de heavenly firmament that goes on foo time
Until de wind decide it got a secret to share
Like it's a friend offering relief from the impregnable heat
Fooling many who began to think all is over
Then Lord-have-mercy!
We started to hear howling, moaning, wailing, screeching, shouting, banging, and ripping
That echoed from the back, scraping and scratching round de walls, and wood, sneaking up windows and doors
It even jumped and pranced atop roofs
Everything started to shudder in fright, crashing against walls, and scurrying to the floor
Even de trees that stood idly by listening and watching everything for hundreds of years, seemed to be taking up root and getting the hell out
of dodge
The enemy was no longer at the gates
Neither were the inhabitants of de Trojan horse now loose to roam at will, and bestow their brand of justice
There was pulling and tearing of galvanize
My God!
The crazy ting was cracking and crumbling walls
Now cat and dogs looked to master as if to say "it's your turn to protect a-we from this all consuming torture reeking havoc on mind and body."

Jesus-have-mercy! You should see de hills and mountains
Once lush they now lay verdant and bare foo miles and miles
Hugo and he friends were like rowdy and destructive teens on
mischief night
Houses looked as though a wrecking ball had flown through them,
they lay in shambles
Bodies of unfortunate animals lay raw and broken, bruised and
bloodied
Getting through your front door was like battling an obstacle course,
or walking through a field filled with land mines
One of Sister Susie's refrigerators was blocking the neighbor's front
door, and everyone knew she house was like Mister Osborne's
showroom
Wedding pictures, paintings, portraits, murals, books, magazines,
pots and pans, televisions, dining and living room furniture
Decorated bushes, roads, and trees, like a church yard bizarre, or an
open flea market
That sleek black jeep de womanizer took out a loan to buy lay twisted
and mangled three quarters of a mile; well correctly put- it in front ah
he three baby-mama, woe-is-me-on-stilts hut; that was still standing
Like de many others just leaning precariously
Mas Joe and Auntie Nan wailing, the prized tamarind, and breadfruit
tree they have treasured, and would kill for, was uprooted
Fields and fields of cane stalk lay trampled, like jumbie had a
bacchanal
I tell you chaos and distress stretch foo miles and miles

Now you listening to stories fact and fiction
This person spending hours wiling, and wilting, shaking, and
shivering, in a closet, under beds, holding on to windows and doors
with rope, in bare hands, or running from one house to the next, to
the next, with the wind wanting to lift them up and carry them away,
like pillaging, plundering, and pilfering pirates
The raindrops felt like soaked leather and razor blades to the skin
Looking around and listening makes you feel as though you are
sucking on a handful of pennies

Your inside bubble and burn, you long to throw up your stomach content
Well come to think of it you do, and nothing comes up anymore, that is after the last three times
And you bawl and bawl, and you pray, and pray some more
Where do I begin?
Good-Lord-up-in-heaven where do we begin?
Why should we dress up; rebuild, repair, scratch and scrounge, save and hoard
When another uninvited guest like Hugo, can just up and decide he or she gonna show its ugly face when it feels the urge

Home

M   Oh so many memories in multitude to recant

O   Of occasions of youth and innocence

N   Numerous and blessed

T   Time has passed yet my love and loyalty remains

S   In songs I sing, speeches I write, stories I tell

E   The essence of my spirit and how easily I

        bounce back from negativity

R   Rarity richness regal resourceful resilient ready repartee

R   Regions rhythms rhymes rhapsody repertoires

        and renditions restorations and renewals replenishing spirit

A   Attention to details attune to every soul's

        whispering with a ready attitude to aid

T   Talent trustworthy true-blue tides foaming and

        furious at the injustice it witnesses to its people

        As the mountains regurgitate spitting up muddy

        rocks hot and oh so scorching

        I see, I hear, I feel, I know, and I will bear everything

        For I am your mount, your terrain, and I will serve

My Place

Little house
Full of chinks full of holes
Rusty leaky roof
With eyes that see everything but tell nothing
Each and every day your weak boards soothe me
I rest my aching head against you
You offer comfort freely
How many emotions you've witnessed
Generations upon generations you have heard about
You were the first to witness the harmony; the union of two unsure souls; lost now
First steps, teardrops, laughter, hurt, joy
Many times I am sure I felt your disapproval in the long slow creaking of every step
I remember how mama use to polish and spit-shine your boards
How she dressed your walls, and cleaned your badly cracked windows
Ours was the smallest, the dingiest in looks
But didn't quite know it then
Even how lucky
Be thankful you've got a place to rest your weary head, hang up your hat, let down your hair
I am your home
Perhaps you will find a better
But never ever forget where you've come from
"Yeah." The trees and bushes around whispered softly bowing their heads
Now tiny creatures make their homes in you inhabiting every crevice
But you have stood your ground, eyed many storms and seen governments change
You've ushered in many years of revolt and even danced in their triumph
How do you know someone asked
I know I said, because no matter what I have done or been through you have stood by in support
So now I know how lucky I am, for the simple fact that I was born in you

Colors of Mind

Green that forever grows, fruitful and fertile
In food for mind, body, heart, soul and spirit
Red that is blessed and remembered
For forgiving atrocities when the life essence spewed from innocent
bodies who just longed for a place to be
Black for pride of a people still not counted by others and even
amongst themselves
You say you are better because your shade is lighter
Much pride is taken in you because your hair is like a doll's; flowing
straight and bouncy
Treated unkindly because you refused to sow seeds of discord
You deserved, you are counted
YOU are SEEN
Yellow for the sunshine and promises, birth and renewal, cleansing
and understanding

Montserrat A Cornucopia of the Senses

The Rock
The Emerald Isle
My Pillow
First Love
The Crush
The Addiction
Teacher, friend, lover
Hopes and dreams
Strength to overcome; oppression and depression
Stresses and starvation of mind and body
Peaceful shore and Haven
Poignant and Bedazzling
An infusion of blood
Commingling of tears and sweat

How about?
Colorful and cantankerous
Sulphuric and boiling
Sunshine and verdant
Pastel and serene
Great Alps and Runaway Ghaut
Festivals and jump-ups
Masquerades and colorful troupes
Sweeping house and yard
Windward Road/George Street and the clash of so-call society
Miss Goosy and Mo Bull
Socca and calypso, unforgettable laureates like Arrow, Reid, Salt fish,
Cut' A, and Brim
Red apple and fry chicken from Red pole
Fashionista's threads from Monkey Eric
Raw cloth from Mercer, Annie Price, and Miss Annie Eid
Banks like Royal and Barclays

Streets like Parliament, and Lovers Lane, not to out do Boobie-Alley and Hag Hole
Then there is Clock Stan/Pier Head/War Memorial/Jetty, or we just say right dong-a-Bay Front
How about an abundance of guava, kinnip, mango, and tamarind, that makes you so stuff you can't sniff a thing else
Lord don't forget market day and marrying produce; some toss, "if you no want um lef um lone, if you no want cuss up you betta lef um dey
Remember babridge and swanks?
Ain't they just as good as ginger beer and sorrel?
Blood pudd'un and Ivy
Petty riots between the Kinsale and the North fellas, settling when Iron band strike
Liming-spots like Evergreen and Nepco Den
How about sports day; green house and red house, even Diamonds and Spades
Remember Sundays of lining up and hollering for Richard Samuel bread?
Get none so you have to go home and settle for floating Suntex delight
Deejays like Basket Ball George, Dubai Richards and Kevin Lewis
Not forgetting the gals with voices; Rose Willock, Molly Campbell, and Juliette Brade
Then there is the infamous S corner, and the only white sand beach Rendezvous
Rip tides at Foxes Bay and Whapping
Dark night Church Road home to cemetery, where many profess they had close encounters with the fearful kind; jumbies
Remember the story of the weary traveler seeking shelter from heavy rain under Church Road tamarind tree, and being serenaded by the sweetest piece of guitar music?
Yeah you remember?
Only to hear the voice say after he paid compliment.
"Suppose you me hear me play when me was alive man."
Lord-have-mercy!!!

Remember Saint Patrick's Day in the South, and St Johns Day in the North
Glendon Hospital and the immortal Nurse Francis
Blackburne Airport gone, now we have Gerald's where car drive underneath and plane taxi pan top
We're moving on up!
Yes Sah! Yes Sah!
Remember Marma Gay, Sally Nan, Red Madge, Crazy Ellen, and Lisa Park?
How about the great crushes who roar about on their dick-sticks; biker dudes like Briggs Morgan, Sydney Charles and Rasta Kenyatta
Clock Stan and carol singing, the cesspool for much political bribery, and where you can be sure of a ride any hour day or night
Teachers; Mini and Estwick, Brown and Taylor
Principals like Dorothy Greenaway and Eddie Babs
Remembering hibiscus and heliconia
Sturge Park, and Woodland's beach
Innocence and daydreaming
First kiss and hand holding
Rain on galvanize roof and starry sky gazing
Coal pits and latrines
Rounders and hopscotch, kudos to those who remember Greenbush/ run and go fetch
See I am remembering you Montserrat
Which is why I can never forget ME

Remembrance and Stressing

Damn Funny Thing about Want

Got one who say he wants you body, mind, and soul
What a friggin laugh eh
Cause you know them ones only come once in a
blue moon
So let's say for reason, or for foolishness sake he wants you with all the
above
Then again that is dangerous territory, you threading on slippery ice
So we will just settle for body
Then again let's not even go there cause we only confusing we self eh
ladies?
Cause damn funny thing about want
You get what you want
Then turns out
Shit!
That ain't what you want
At all, at al, at all

I Feel the Urge

What does she have that I don't seem able to give you
To make you yearn for me in that all so consuming way
Is it the voice?
Does it irritate you?
Is it because I don't come across as being helpless?
Is it that my chest is to big, and the ass to flat?
Or is it because I don't fall and fawn enough at your feet?
How about not hanging on to your every word?
Or let you spread my legs as far as the divide between whites and
blacks, or colored people on a whole?
Shit! Listen up!
Is it because I keep my mouth clamp shut while you turn my insides
to mush?
So I don't hurt your feelings by telling you, you aren't rocking my
world like you think?
Claiming there is nothing new out there that anyone can teach you
about your so call sexual performance;
that leaves me wanting to rewind, touch and pleasure myself
Or perhaps reach for my Man-dingo-battery-operated-bad-boy;
gathering dust in my night stand
Because your baby ego will definitely be bruised
Giving you reasons to go creeping about like some cat burglar
Climbing up on anything in de alley who would suck your little dick
for a price
I mean what has she got that I don't?
Perhaps is it because I don't let it all hang out
Call you a motherfucker, a two timing-heart- stomping-commitment
phobic-yellow belly-serpent crawling-night creeping-lying-cheating-
no good-bull shitting-no action-a one minute-mama's boy
Tell me what has she got that I haven't?
There is a saying; one hand can't clap, nor two fingers make a fist
Got me?
It shouldn't be all one sided here

So I am telling you now that I am tired
I am so god-damn tired of you and all your shit
Tired of staying at home pretending not to be waiting for your call
Living a half-ass existence sort of life
Chatting up a lazy Tom, an ugly Dick, and a fat and greasy Harry
Just to get you to realize I exist
I mean come on already
You chicken liver-no going down dey-pussy-hater
Tell me man, what has she got that I haven't?

You/Tainted Love

She promised that she wasn't ever going to talk about you
She was going to file you away with all those troublesome secrets
That somehow you always managed to get her talking about
Seeing as she wore her tongue on her sleeves when it came to you
Must have told you everything
That is why for the love of God she couldn't understand why you still called her a liar
Then again is it not the pot calling the kettle black?

You said there was nothing you two couldn't talk about
Ha! Ha!
She didn't learn
Guess it was all one sided
So the laughs are on her
For the silly school girl crush and the naiveté
Looking up with head in the clouds, and eyes on the sun
When she should have kept those beautiful pools of brown glued to you
You the master manipulator, you lying cheating commitment phobic chicken-livered ass
Yes if the cap fits mister
That is way she wouldn't have missed you skipping by her heart and puncturing her soul
Learning ways to cut and bruise her body and mess with her heart

Now she is there missing you something awful
She said there is a burning, and a tightening in her chest
Heart burn she surmised you would say, as she clutched her chest tightly
But I think it is her yearning for you
She misses hearing your voice, listening to you laugh, and you singing those silly ditties, as you rambled on

She looks like she wants to weep; I reach out for her, and hold her tightly until the moment passed
She is fighting the urge; she says if she starts there would be no end
Now wouldn't you like to be a sneaky little creepy fly on the wall?
To have a great laugh at her expense
What the hell did she ever see in a weak SOB like you?

She is freaking, wondering what the hell she did that was so wrong
So wrong to drive you so far away, and send you packing
Distance, she is crying
Wondering how could speaking to each other for twenty years create such distance?
And so many prayers and whispered apologies not mend this rift
Silly really, how very silly I say every time I see the way you ignore her
Or listen to the promises she makes; like she would never allow anyone ever again to get that close
But that is cheating I say to her
Giving up on life
Giving up on living and being the best her, and for who, someone like you?
I am afraid you are not worth it my friend
She could do so much better
So you will not win, you cannot, I will not let you
So I've said to her to forget you
Forget shit, wipe her feet, toss the shoe and move on
Get on with the task of living and loving
It was just so sad that you played her and no doubt yourself
She could have been the best thing that happened to YOU

Idiotic Child

Why can't you let go of that idiotic child that God made
Who just seems to be getting on with his life?
Leaving you wanting, worrying, hoping, stressing, longing, and
fussing
Your emotions are going up and down like a yoyo for this
cantankerous being
That makes you want to lie down and have yourself a long cry
But what if you can't stop; put a cork on it?
Especially when a huge part of you doesn't think he deserves any of it
Why were you so blind to see girl
To hear exactly what he was saying
Guess you are learning now that words are just words without actions
For anyone can say I love you/I care for you
But what should keep you from that person you claim to care for and
love
When he or she is sick and in need
From checking in most times
Give more than just single syllables
No small insignificant lies white or otherwise
No excuses
Jesus why can't you just let go of this idiotic child the Lord made
Who turns and twists you
Kicks and abuse your emotions
Tramples on your caring
Leaves you out there to hang in the wind by nothing but your
fingernails
There are days when your emotions are so delicate
So much so that one word, a song, a gesture could tear you up
To the point where people stop and stare, like you should really have
yourself committed
Instead you are home snatching and ripping pictures and things
collected
Sniffling and burying your face and nose into folds of a lifetime

Dying and birthing
Repeating the cycle
Hurting and suffocating
Succumbing and praying
For a lifeline
Wishing you were a boozer
Only a broken spirit is crying out, "Stay away"
For it is just another idiotic thing just like him

Silent Screams

You bark and growl your angry words
Touching grabbing stroking
Fanning the flames of your desire
I scream no! Stop! Help!
But it falls on deaf ears
For without permission you take, and take, and take
You touch for pleasure rejoicing in my pain
Criticizing, belittling, punching, poking, prodding Incessantly you
run amuck in head and heart

Ode to Yesterday

Sometimes it's like I have never been, never met you
Had you hold me in your arms and whispered in my ears, kiss my
lips, and caress my body
Learning most all my secret, intimate, treasured, used, abused,
broken, soiled, moist, tender, forgiving, torture-some, fearful,
yearning
Lord have mercy
Lord have mercy
I had better start forgetting
Forgetting meeting you and being in your arms, tick
Forgetting being lied to on so many occasions, tick
Forgetting the fiery trails blazed, that are still smoldering
I can hear the locks clanging shut
Keys jangling clicking as they enter holes
Bones are withered, and waiting to be scattered

Layers/ Rose Petals & Onion Rings

He told you he couldn't commit couldn't give you what you wanted
Neither what you needed
Basic survival in this trying game of love
Misuse and abuse criticism condescension
Each day I allowed you to peel layer after layer
Exposing me raw leaving me bare
Maybe tomorrow is the constant prayer on my lips
Lord you have some serious 'splaining to do
Ultimatums resolutions
Maybe I should kiss your ass
How about become a trapeze lover with the stamina of a race horse
Devotion subjugation
Abandoning priorities procrastinating
Becoming a carbon copy of one of those chicken-headed beauties
Whose mantra is why, why, why
When I just simply let you

Signs

Should have known you'd walk all over my heart
As though it were years old concrete
When you laughed in my face when I told you
It's fragile
It's worn
It's torn
Gathered up and stitched together by the skilful hands of
Timidity
Self-doubt
Mistrust
Great friendships
Many sleepless nights
Comfort foods
Praying
Begging
Lying
Weeping and wailing
Overwork
Shopping
Reading
Journaling
Laughing
Daydreaming
Wanting
Wishing
Hoping
Dreaming and believing
That next time I can spot him first before he does me

Fate and all that Karmic Shit

Ever made a promise like; not gonna think about him?
Well not so much, or probably not at all
Not even gonna call
Not gonna sit by the telephone
Not gonna answer when he calls
Well not on the first ring, second, or third
"Hello!" She pants
Sucker!

Not gonna think about what we were doing yesterday and the day
before
It was raining
It was sunny
It was snowing
When we were at the movie
Walking down the street and you reached for his hand when a vamp-
on-the-prowl passed by
With her 'do' just right, and ass so tight, and chest just
Lord have mercy!
And low-and-behold he squeezed it back
The man had the nerve to reassure; looking deep within your eyes.
Silly you, you thought God must love you
When all the while he probably needed support; a leash for his
trifling-roaming-dog-like-ass

How about not gonna spend another red-cent buying him anything
But he made you feel oh so-so-so good
He turned your ass out
So you gonna buy him this and that
Oh my baby gonna look so good
You picture it in your mind's eye
So you get him this and that and then some more

Forgetting that rent gonna come skippity-hoppity around the corner,
leaving you to wonder how you gonna pay
Seeing he ain't even giving you a penny, not even a dime to rub
together
So you put in some overtime
Now you more tired than a mother-f*****
More tired than de donkey that carried Mary
But you are gonna go home and cook, clean, wash, and iron, and
give him the best oops!
Good girls don't talk like that
So you perform like Angela Basset winning Miss Halle's award
Yet you get nothing, nothing, and nothing in return
So you promised you are gonna teach him a lesson
Then suddenly there is that silly song that sets up residence in your
head like a moocher
And gets tears and self pity to sign in
They are room mates from the abyss
Seems like you can't get rid of them for shit
Raining on your gonna-be-a-stronger-me-sistah-parade
And as if you haven't suffered enough
Here comes Fate in his pushy ass
Keep putting you and him in places and situations
Even in your own space; you reach for a book and oops, there is his
picture
You go rummaging in the not-so-sexy part of your
underwear drawers, and his silly face stares up grinning
How about all those letters you thought you tore up or burned
The cheap-ass memorabilia's
Tears, self pity, and stupidity comes hippity-skippity
Then stupidity yells out for you to call him
Now excuse is calling out, "got room for me?"
Meanwhile he is asking "why are you calling me?"
Shit! Shit! Shit!
She squeezed out, banging the telephone against a most throbbing
head
He stomped you dead once again

Teach Me

You said you had to get to know her
Talk to her, learn what makes her tick
Think you can?
Think the interview went well?

She doesn't like liars who say they will call and don't
She doesn't like people who kiss and tell
She definitely wouldn't give you a piece on the first date
But wait a second!
You haven't even asked her out on any
Yet you tried to get into her pants
Shame on you!
Shame on her!
For good girls try to hold out for six months
Well three months tops the experts say
But she confesses; she would have given you a piece on the first night
What!
Okay, okay…
But he hasn't given her cause to

She heard he is sick
She pictures herself like Florence Nightingale
Rushing to his hospital bed to nurse him back to health
But guess what she doesn't know exactly which hospital
She doesn't even have an address for where he claimed he lives
She scrambled about for telephone numbers, and called leaving
messages
To this day she is still waiting for him to say he heard at least one
Shame on you!
Shame on her!
For making promises she hasn't kept
Wishing and praying for what though?
What is this lesson that she has to learn?

That you are teaching and she hasn't grasp?
Open your heart, open your mind
Stop being made a fool of
Trusting wholeheartedly in a fantasy
Wake up my sistah, and learn what he has already majored in
PLAYAH!
But don't hate him
Hate the game we all play

How Do You Say

N. A. T. O. (No Attention to the Obvious)
This is a big day for a Summit Meeting
Cause lately she has been feeling brave
She can feel 'it' when his breath touches her skin
As his lazy ass lay sleeping up in her bed, snoring loudly
She longs to place the pillow over his face and keep it there
Especially when she thinks of the numerous times he's shit in her
toilet and leaves skids as a parting gift
Then he pays her no attention
None at all, not even to Miss Mary; dry and aching, because the
television gets more foreplay from him
She grimaced as she recalls how he rushes to pluck the biggest piece of
chicken of the plate
Telling you, "your gonna thank me one day baby, especially seeing
how big you are getting round there; he touches your tummy
No babies remember? He grins stupidly, pointing a skinny claw-like
finger across to her
She wanted to huff, "who in de hell do you think constantly buys the
damn condoms asshole?"
Here are some other things that has her panties wrapping tighter
around her neck
His irritating chewing, his loud voice, and crass laughter
Look he says, pulling her out of her reverie
How do I say this babe?
Look I am just not feeling you, I am not feeling us." He tossed with
such flair and dripping sarcasm
All eyes turned and zeroed in like a heat sinking missile to its target;
her
She smiles sweetly, admonishing him to keep his voice down
After all she can't let every Tom, Dick, and Harry sift through their
dirty laundry tossed out in the street
It leaves her feeling like he just kicked and trampled her in the gut
with government boots

Recovery time is taking longer than she wants, to the point where he
is up and walking away
No he didn't! She thought, anger bubbling like festering lava
No! That stinking-ass, free-loading, cheapskate-son-of-a-bitch!
She is feeling like she's standing naked in a crowded room with
everyone pointing
She wants a big hole to open up and swallow her
How could she have allowed things to get this far?
When did this puppy dog grow up and become such a ferocious
bitch?
How could she allow this scab to belittle her in front of everyone?
To have her wanting to scurry and scramble under the table
She covers her face with trembling hands
Lord have mercy
Lord have mercy
It didn't happen did it
He never said what he did, did he?
"Babes!"
He is back
Her hands come down, her heart is confused; it is pumping, jumping,
stomping, flying, crumbling
She dared to look up, as the twins cowardly galloped up; Hope and
Expectancy
Maybe he had a change of heart they sang, because you know that it
is damn hard to find a man out there these days
"Sorry babes"
"Yes! Yes!" Her heart soared
"Do you have a twenty? I need to pay for the cab."
The balls!!!
Pity he didn't use them in the time they were together
Saliva churned and bubbled to the top as she riffled
through her pocket and purse in confusion
Then suddenly it hits her
Everything came rushing back
She is now hotter than a rooster in a hen house as a thought suddenly
slapped her in the face

She reached for the fiver that winked up mischievously from the table top
She smiled and picked it up and handed it over
"By the way take this five, maybe you can earn the rest the good-old-fashion way. Sadly I doubt it, cause babe I didn't feel yah. Know what I mean? And I definitely don't mean us."

Poison Pen on Men by Miss Hurt & Fed-up

What in the world prompts men to make the choices they do?
No really
Especially in picking those females that drape off their arms like ill-
formed appendages
Not to forget dumping you when you do all the shit that's supposed
to count in the crazy relationship
Like not cheating on his big-fat-black-obnoxious ass
When he gives damn nothing but a stab with that short stumpy dick
You get ready, but oops!
He's already done
Then he rolls off, and over, blowing like a beached whale
Thinking he did something fucking awesome; like scaling Mount
Everest on his ears

She learned that silence is golden when it comes to bedroom antics
for you crazy ass-bastards
Except when you are pounding away at a female's body
Whipping yourselves into a psychotic frenzy
Asking all the while, "Feel me? Feeling me baby?"
So for peace of mind, and to end the torture she says
 "Yes baby! Yes baby!"
Once she even tried to offer a bit of couching
Go left, slow, slow, faster, faster, give me more…
The fool stopped, and rolled off, couple seconds later he deflated,
limp as an overcooked noddle
She was starved for months, he couldn't find his mojo, or so he
claimed
He blamed her, and she humbled and stroked an ego that was
apparently growing bigger, and oh so damn meaner
To the point of spewing viciousness
Especially when accepting bullshit 'stroking'

You are not like the one I told you about he bragged one day like a
pussy-whipped-sucker
Who never catered to his every need
Oh shit! Hold up! That's it!
Yes told her many times about Miss Thing
He told her for years about the number one bee
Yet she closed her eyes and ears, and opened her legs and heart
Yes she allowed him to take her body on a test run; a long joy ride for
years
Letting him rev the engine, put his foot down and pushed the gears
Then screeched suddenly to an abrupt halt
He didn't want to drive the car anymore
It's old and worn he said, he needed a new one
She recalled a saying; get what you want, you really didn't want it
How about the guilt trips
To the point where she started to believe the madness
Thinking she's said one thing, after he'd convinced her otherwise
Especially when she got the urge to let her fingernails do a type of
sand-paper-drive-by on his disruptive face
Even snake out those lying cheating-deceptive eyes

Lies, lies, and more lies
About him, her, even herself; the worst deception of all
Because if she could hurt herself so badly, inflict such emotional
wounds with such conviction
Conceive and compose a lifetime novella on no tomorrows and a
sketchy past
She moaned, it was to pathetic to think about
Girl you need a damn lobotomy on head and heart
Just so you could grow some balls and toss his ass to the curb
Forget him like he has so obviously done to you

Now she's awaiting a hopeful future
Where she would see him walking the streets like a madman
Because Miss Thing was through biting, chewing, and spitting his
sorry ass out
He had it coming, yes you have it coming lover

She yearned to see this happen
So she would get a chance to spit in his contriving-no-good-lying face
See him hurt, humiliated, broken, and destroyed
Left with nothing but a broken spirit
She wondered would she lift a finger to help?
That was what her heart dared to ask
She wondered if she could be unforgiving, cold, calculating, and heartless
He would deserve it
Since he didn't deserve her and everything she gave openly and with such trust

Laughter broke forth from the deepest regions of her heart
She laughed like a mad women
I've got you, and I've got it now!
I've got it now my friend
Ha! Ha!
Finally I've got it
So watch out Mister
It could be days and weeks
Seconds and minutes
Months and years
Even moments
But here is the guarantee, the strongest belief
Your turn is coming
Oh yes your turn is coming
Then somehow I will find the strength to laugh, and spit in your heartless and willful face
Mark those words, for your day is coming
One day we will most definitely have the last laugh
Sincerely Miss Hurt, and Miss Fed Up

The Elusive

Yes! Oh yes!
Right there!
Yes! Right there!
Yes! Yes! Yes!
Ooh! Ooh! Ooh!
Yes! Yes! Yes!

Believe that?
Well we've got a parcel of land to sell you in the Sahara
And contrary to popular belief or in the immortal words of our dear
friend Samantha of Sex and the City
F*** me! F*** me! F*** me!!!!

However not to many of us are in the mood
To many things running rampant through the mind
Am I a size 10? Shit I am a 16
Are my breasts beginning to reach my ankles?
My behind; is there two cheeks or four
Am I firm or soggy in all the right places?
If I give him now will I see him tomorrow?
Did I take my birth control?
This morning, last night, yesterday
Will the neighbors think me a hoochie-mama when they witness
Tito, or was it Sam
Shit! Shit! Shit!
She screwed up again
Or was it Thomas leaving this morning
What will he think, they think, if I suggest condoms?
No maybe he'll think me a 'whore'
Is this going to be child number two or four?
Is he going to stick around to help take care of it
Or is he going to run and say "wasn't me"
Where was his dick?

What ocean was it swimming in the last 24hrs?
And on and on it goes
For maybe 55% of the female populous
But what happens to the other 45% who long to touch the hem of
the ever so elusive?
What's that?
Well the answer is the big O; the elusive ORGASM

Phoenix

That face
Jarring
Those eyes
Piercing
Like you are searching soul and probing mind
Those lips
Delicious and succulent
Them there hands
Stroking and fanning
Dear lord where does she begin
Not forgetting that knee-trembling and hand-shaking smile
Or that dick!
That dick that makes her hit those high everlasting notes Oooh!!!
She is remembering
She is recalling
But funny though when the clouds part and the sun shines through,
and she opens her eyes
Open those eyes girlfriend
A piece of ass is just that, a piece of ass
You were one of the things on his to do list
Especially if you were up there; his mind's pin up poster girls
Another conquest, another notch on his headboard, on his belt
So it's crying time again, back to the drawing board
Step back regroup; gather your troupes
You are beaten now girlfriend
But a time will come
When you will forget that face
That face that makes you think of the crumbling Twin Towers
A pile up on the George Washington Bridge
Or the Blizzard of 1989

Oh those eyes.
Measuring and calculating
Devious shifty and trifling
That smile
She is looking away
For not all skin-teeth is a smile
Not all that glitters gold
But she will forget you
When she looks at herself in the mirror and not turn away to wipe
tears
When she says yes to that extra shift and crawls out of bed and tosses
the covers
When she says no to that other trifling fool with your exact eyes, lips,
and smile
And yes again to your redeemer
Oh yes!
When she grabs a few moments of happiness
And yes peace of mind for her self
For she will be a bit older and wiser in most of the ways it counts
And she will forget you
Oh yes she will forget you

Stupid Stupid/ Eggs in a Leaky Basket

Of all the stupid hair-brain gutless spineless things to do
Sent you a message, you ignored it
Called you, but you hustled me off the telephone
You claimed you are sort of busy
"So are you going to call me back?"
"Yes I will."
"When?"
"Later."
"Later when?"
"When I am through."
So I wait and waited, and waited some more
I am still waiting

Now it's a brand new year
The telephone rings, I rushed to it
Only disappointment
Still don't get it huh girlfriend?
Then say it with me.
He doesn't give a fuck about you; he is just not into you
He is all about one thing
Me and me and more me
He is a man after all
Fucking you till I get my fill then I move on to the next gullible
female
You and You and You
And yes You

Why so surprise?
Told you exactly who I am
Yet you chose not to believe
So why blame me for taking what you so readily gave up without
pause
Just because I flattered you with a few cultured words

Brandished a wad of cash in your face
Took you out a couple of times to Sizzlers instead of Burger King
Bought you a rose even though it was wilted
Like my attention after I got into your panties
Under your skin
Let me ask again
What did I do that was so wrong?
After all you put your heart and soul on a golden platter
Told me to eat and fill up as I chose
Knowing full well I wasn't honest
Could never be
Not even with the others
I mean how incredible gullible of you
Fooling yourself into thinking we were friends
Even after I told you not to put all your eggs in my basket
Opening your heart like a heavy jacket on a semi-cool sunny day in
winter
Now you blame me knowing I am a typical male; having the hots for
anything in a short skirt and high heels
Well shame on me for not wanting to f*** it! F*** you!
Oops!

You think you got me huh
You called me gay
Yeah fucking happy and hilarious
The big joke is on you.
Yeah you
It is you
I am fucking anything that slithers and right under your nose
Because you are stupid, stupid, stupid
Oh well
Better you than me

Colors of Body

Translucent tears ran down a feverish and raging body
A mind in so much chaos
How could you go from saying I love you mere moments ago
In sweet kisses and unforgettable hugs
To spell out now
You are nothing in my eyes
I hate you, and I never want to see you again
In the purple welts that tingled across face, breast, torso; front and
back, legs
Reminders in black and blue bruises, from caramel and kola nut,
chocolate and sun burnt leather, midnight and sienna; fists
The world is no longer just simply a white and black issue/race of
people raging against each other
Causing the yellow to ooze and stink, and the red to gush and splatter
White is tainted and stained, and yes black is cracking
 Especially if we no longer know or hold respect for anything
Nothing is sacred anymore
Things are pulled down, trampled upon, roughed up and fucked up
So you are shocked?
The phrasing makes you uncomfortable
You are uneasy?
Okay, well now that I've got your attention, then maybe we are ready
to come together and begin again
Start a new revolution, a new world order

Resilience & Thanks

Mother

They come in different shapes, sizes, and color
Faces that change with every mood
Some will hug and kiss you
Others will just let you
Smiling face with twisted heart
A face that refuses to smile its undaunted
One that smells of the expense of the world
Another that smells of a hard day of work; curry and furniture polish
One who struts her stuff down the runway blowing you a kiss from
some far off adventure
One who can't find the strength to get out of bed, or up from in front
of the television
One who lost her rights unjustly to some cruel twist; an eye maybe
both to see how high you can fly
She can't hear you call her mama, but if you look at her she can read
your lips
She is locked away in some jail cell; she tried to protect you
Or some idiot saw fit to steal her right to walk this earth
Her choice snatched away simply taken; gone
She stands before a classroom and pours her heart out that by the
time she gets home she has nothing but impatience left for us
On the other hand she does nothing at all and still has no time except
to call out, "bring me that bottle over there you, and scowl I can't
stand the sight of you. You rotten child cursed with the face of the
most cruel man I know."
Then you watched her drown herself with white rum or scotch, down
pill after pill losing count, injecting some calm into her veins with a
lethal poison
She is white as alabaster against my dad and myself; as brown as
crushed cinnamon, or black as a starless sky
There are so many more to add to the list
But which one is she?
Can you pick your mother?

Ma Baby

He stood towering; mountainous and without compunction
Arms raised and gnarled like wintry skeletons
Fist; that mere seconds ago painted harsh ugly images on face; eyes
mouth and jaw
There was no strength left to fend him off of his daily diatribe and
weekly torture
Isolation and misery became confidants
Makeup, alcohol, and neck-and wrist clothing to cover up from
friends
Fast forgot what a good day felt like when seconds wild away into
minutes, hours, days, weeks, and years
Such a miserable and wasted existence this life I live
Then one day like a phoenix you rose up from the ashes
With the fear of the almighty perched high atop your shoulder
That precocious jut in your angular chin and with a voice like a
heavenly orchestra resounding you said
"God-dammit! Not my baby!"

Up and up the ladder men seem to climb leaving us crumpled and
bruised
We get lost in the daily shuffle, affirming no compromising of self as
a mantra
So you work to the best of your ability
That when you sleep the sleep and walk the walk
You my baby can hold your head high
Like Cleopatra and Queen Tiye, and so many other Nubian queens
I heard your voice calm, clear, and prideful say
"Oh no you don't, not my baby."

In passing I heard one of your brother's call a sister a bitch
I wanted to snatch his lips, and tear them from the face and trample
them
But I think I am only one, programmed to think weak

So I walk on by, that is until another had the audacity to want to give me a dressing down filled with profanities
"Who do you think you are?"
With pride burning and coursing fiercely in my veins, I say, "Your mother, your sister, blood and mirror image."
I done preaching my baby

Lesson 1 + 2 and Rewind

Didn't have much growing up
Scarcity and meanness was plenty
Love and happiness few
Prayed so hard to grow up
Made a vow; to make a difference

I would meander through fancy neighborhoods
Where it seems all fantasies became reality
Nothing was left to chance
The beautiful with the rich
The sexy-fighting-wannabe's trying to gain the attention of the haves

I am grown now and blessed with a good job and much money
Want things they are at the fingertips
I have become Mrs. Midas
Well known and respected for miles
Living it up in one of those long-sort-after mansions
This is living and I have arrived world
Yet something is amiss

Suddenly I have come to the stark reality that over the years
There are no little feet to greet, no one to call me mommy
To fight for my attention and look upon me in expectation
For the great deceiver; time; is against me
It seemed in all the haste to grow up and succeed
I have forgotten the truth to living
Extensions; extensions matter, they are the gifts we e leave behind

Now here I am playing catch-up
However the body has wandered off
The bio-clock has stopped
I am now left exhausted
As I seek ways to produce the greatest achievement
YOU

A Note to Mama

Hello Mama
Dear Mama
How do I begin?
Where do I begin?
Oh yes!

The baby, our baby that you have never seen
What a tremendous waste, a crying shame really
Mama I wish you could see her
The way her eyes light up like a million fire flies dancing in the
island's breeze on a dark night
Like sunbeams on snowflakes
Mama she is happy and has not a care in the world
Guess who she reminds me of?
Her long graceful arms, her hands, her fingers when they flail in the
air reaching out to me
Her touch asks no questions, and shows no trepidation
Mama our baby is beautiful and kind
Come see her, come see me
Forgiveness is not bought it is earned
Well earning is learning mama wouldn't you say?
I learn each day from her that love can move mountains set you free
This epiphany I yearn to share with you
She is a miracle, she is our miracle
So what do you say?
Meet us halfway?

Sun kissed

Up the sun came peering out from among dew stained leaves
Freshly kissed, and alive with yet another blessed breath
The Lord smiles well on us this morning you will always say
Watering the creepers, plucking here, pruning there
Busily your long brown fingers disappeared in the cold damp sweet
smelling earth
The sweetest smile would caress your ethereal face
The creases and lines on your brown skin knows lots of joy and flirted
with pain
Experienced miracles, and danced with fame
How do you do it?
Make the stars shine brighter, the heaven seeming nearer
Farfetched dreams attainable fought without fear?
Gradually darling
Put one foot ahead of the other, with one step at a time
One for you, and one for the heavenly father
Live life to its fullest, and have no regrets
And above everything else my dear child
Open up your heart
Let it soar
Let it fly
Never forget to love

Island Mama

Trees of green swaying in the cool island breeze
Like you mama
You know the way your eyes wandered off to some distant view only
you alone could see
Then you returned with your words of wisdom putting us at ease

The black sand glitters under the heat of the searing sun
Waves shimmering dancing rushing to open-armed shores
You would always say
Never be afraid to reach for a dream
Always fight hard for what you want

I see your strength like the endless fields of white cotton
Fighting the winds, braving all the elements
Fighting for their right to survive
Just like you mama

Oppression, depression, segregation
You fought for a right for us to be
Walk with pride head held high
High like the tall coconuts
Do not forget how many triumphs
Fought with blood sweat and tears they have seen
Smell the fury as the volcano opens up to make its presence known
Its sulphuric belly bubbles and burns in vengeance
For us now and for those past

This poem is for both my mothers, and the pride they hold for me. I see it, I hear it, and I feel it.

Night and Day

Like an angel, and like a beacon, these two stand
One on either side
Whispering, encouraging, reassuring, scolding, beseeching, prompting
Child of mine, child of ours, you must go on, press on
The victory is not yours, not ours, not theirs
Don't give your energy to those who don't stop to listen
To those who don't appreciate you for who you are
Don't give time to haters who do nothing but flap jealous gums, and try to dig ditches for you to fall into
Brush off those who take viciousness to your body, and try to wound your heart
Shake those off who will always try to pound you repeatedly into the ground, and try to turn you to dust with a deceiving look, a greedy hand, or ill-mannered voice
Be a phoenix child and rise, rise up from the ashes, do it over and over
Pause long enough to smell the poignancy of creativity, and revel in authenticity
You are my beauty, you are my voice
You are my boosting, you are our uplifting
You are my extension, you are the North Star
You listened to my story of abuse; you even bore witness to some
You learned what to stand for, and speak out against

You my girl knows what you will take from others, and when to say
enough and simply walk away
You will call to say mama I am here
Mama listen, look, see how high I have flown
You will say good on you my girl, good on you for taking the courage
to do what I couldn't
What I was to afraid to reach out and grasp
Because of what I forced self to internalize
Stunting and stifling growth because others said I shouldn't, I
couldn't, or who told you that you had the balls to say yes I can

You go my girl; take our underlying strength, all our blood sweat and
tears
Make your mark, carve out a place for those coming behind who
think they can't, or shouldn't
I was happy when I gave myself, and so afraid when I felt helpless to
make a place for you
I wanted to sing, I wanted to walk the runway dressed like an island-
goddess, and have many adore me
But I didn't get the push
The feet failed, and one excuse turned into two, three, until I was
crippled
First by my thoughts, then his, then others and I didn't try
Fear kept me so caged that at times I think I tried to force it upon
you
Thank God you did not listen my girl
You refused to be stuffed in a box, and pushed away
My God I look at you my girl, we look at you to see anything of us
Sometimes in your beauty we glimpse a touch of fear in those dreamy
eyes
What dreams you have to the point where we want to say shut your
mouth, because they wouldn't let you
But what gives me the right, what gives us the right
What gives them the right?
Talents are not ours to dispense, for our Creator gives and takes

Now look at you my knock-kneed beauty
You are like a gazelle in the tilt of your chin, the span of your eyes
Listen to the eloquence of your speech, its like nothing I gave or even
encouraged
Others may phew and say its nothing but putting on airs
But I say, we say, you go girl, give them something to talk about
Because I rejoice when I see you walk into a room and all eyes
automatically turn to you
You go girl! Cause you sure done make something of yourself
You dreamed big, and reached out for your bit of sky
You will sure leave your mark, it will never be erased
Others will find the guts to say she did, so we definitely can
My girl I didn't get all the questions you asked
Why you always wrote everything down, and scribbled on the walls,
and marked the floors
I noticed, we noticed
You were always so silent and watching, weaving, implementing,
stitching, smiling, and ruminating

Deep water, sleeping dog, you both used to say
I laughed, and I still laugh even now
For little did you both realized that I am just as you both are;
extensions of a unique blend of two very powerful forces
You are night, and she is day

Reflections

Came home in a huff; heart pounding, winged feet, flying tongue
"Mama! Mama! Guess what!"
Then like a bolt of lightning it hits me yet again
Like a swift kick in the gut
You are no longer here mama
You are not here to greet me; with that smile spread from ear to ear,
With arms cast wide that will hold me tight until I decide to step out
of safety

Up the drive we would walk hand in hand as I tell you things that
happened throughout the day
Things that were not so good you say will get better
Especially after a good meal, and a great night of sleep
But Mama I slept for days, and ate like a horse
Yet you did not come
You did not come mama
My heart bleeds, and my soul burns

I am remembering that Christmas
When all we had for our tree was thread, and cut out pictures and
burnt popcorn
But we stayed up all night dying and stringing
We called it our little tree of color and love
Never was there one more lovelier
Something else that hasn't left me; how did you do it
How did you raise me?
How did I make it this far?
But look!
Look at me now!
I made it!
I am flying!

I am flying mama!
Really flying!
Look!
See!
Look see how high I am flying mama?

Contradictions of a Mother

M   Motivating, mentoring, moaning, ministering, misunderstood, meeting, multi-talented. My own special someone who stands by me no matter what

O   Ownership, oozing, open, opposing, opposite, offending, oppressive, opinionated
    We owe everything to you, all praise and even some put downs

T   Tough, together, tentative, touchy, tender, true, treatment, teetering, tearful, tense, trustworthy, turbulent, tricky, true-blue, and teaching of self.

H   Heaven, honest, heartbreak, helper, home maker, healer, humble
    Having a heart, taking in everything that hurts and humiliate

E   Everlasting, equal, essence, eclectic, expendable, expandable, earthy, endearing. You are electricity pumping through veins, giving will to persevere when all else fails

R   Rendering, receiving, resistant, reaching, rich, resourceful, revolving in lessons in realism
    She is the pillow and anchor, giving arms as refuge

S   Sisterhood, saint, selfish, seeking, slave, sensitive, skin, superwoman, storm, savior
    Seeing eye for all, ship's captain, and the soul of everything I am, or ever hope to become

Heart of Mine

Would I honor you?
Uplift you in praise?
Or foist upon you limits that others enforce?
I pray I never fail you
That I never cause you harm
That I am around to protect when monsters come a prowling
That I am blessed with the balm to soothe
Child of mine
Heart of mine
Even though inhabitants have been sometimes cruel
And I question my purpose
My very way of being my plan
I miss that you are not here to see me soar
Or whisper I am so very proud of you
Or an I miss you my love, on the breeze that blows its sweet heavenly
lullaby
My hope, my future, my one bright star
In this often times hateful universe
Where people enter and exit so quietly and often times under
unnoticing eyes
In a moment, in a space of time
Come fresh mist of morning
Caress my sad tired soul
Breathe in me hope
In every smile kiss and warm embrace
Every exchange without your presence
Mother of mine
Heart of mine
For there you will live on always
Each moment
Every memory
A time, a breathe, a touch
My mother, my love, my friend, my everything

Insights & Fantasy

Miss Sandra Dee & Mr. So-and-So

Girls night out
Time to unwrap that hair, pull out that little black dress, and call up
all your dead to rally about
You want to look F I N E- Fantastic, Incredible, Naughty as you
Enter!
Venue; the G-Spot
Uh huh
Motto; If it moves snatch it, lie down jump it, lean you f*** it
Really! Truly! I kid you not

Not to long after being seated, and we placed our orders; Virgin Pina
Colada twice
Can't handle the heavy stuff she said to her girls
But now she's rethinking her choice.
Especially with the amount of girl power diatribe flitting about the
table
It was enough to make a hard dick cower like a priest in confession
So the need arose for some much needed fresh air
Plus she had to wash that man; Mr. Waiter-man
Oops!
To late can't take it back!
For truly Mr. Waiter-man was drop-dead-gorgeous
The name the girls came up with for Mr. Waiter-man was Mr. Labia-
curling-teeth-sweating-knee-jerking-well hung...
All eyes seemed riveted to the spot
Hers drifted for fear, to his feet
She couldn't help but recall some sayings
Cold hands, warm heart
Big feet, big d***
You truly are getting warmer
Well back to the story.

Needless to say Mr. Waiter-man had all the ladies
panties in a twist
The sistahs were bonkers; they were going out of their minds
Sistah over there; skirt so short could have been a noose for her neck
Sistah there with the legs sprouting from her armpits, eyed him like a
gravy-smothered pork chop
You couldn't forget the fella with the voice higher than Michael
Jackson's hee-hee
How about that moon-walking brother?
Hold up!
Damn!
It's a sistah!
Hell no!
That's a dude!!!
He stepped sweeter than a cat on a hot tin roof
There was another chick more plentiful than roses in May and June,
smelling like she took a bath steeped in cinnamon, after being thrown
off the set of Planet of the Apes
Better yet like she was Sasquatch's mama
Had to get some air before bacchanal broke out in the G Spot

Well hello there
Came from out of the wall she was leaning against
"Talking to me?" She asked, and pointed to herself when her heart
settled from jumping to the diamond clad firmament
"Of course I am talking to you Miss Shy-star, drinking only virgin-
slush. How about something hard and stiff?"
"Right here, right now?"
 Oops!
 She couldn't take it back; no bolting the barn door to call animals
back to roost, once you left the door open
But the prissy-shoe-up-the-butt-nose-in-the-air-look-at-me-I-am-
Sandra-Dee bullshit mamas love to drill into the brains of their young
girls/females
Just so they can acquire a cheap-ass piece of gold; that enables a man
to wreak havoc on her psyche
Save yourself sistah-friend, and let's hear an Amen!

Well back to the story
Do you know Mr. Waiter-man had the nerve to cheekily toss back,
well if you'd like, just say the word
Sahara! She thought, not realizing she had said it out loud
That long huh? He snatched it and threw back, and the next thing
she knew
Her feet, and hand had come together and mingled with scorching
hot breath
She sucked on his sugar lumps as though they were the fount of life's
essence
She tossed all hope for sense and sensibility
They scampered away like bandits
She was Jezebel wrapped in Miss Maya's Phenomenal Woman
Oh God yes!
Phenomenal Woman! That's me! She yearned to shout
She breathed like a marathon runner
Her body was in such an abandoned and rhapsodious and most
delightful state
Her well-manicured French tips grazed, brushed, caressed and left a
blazing fiery trail wherever they wandered
She bucked and reared
She wished and hoped
She enjoyed and prayed
Lord let him not be another twat-tickler, or a plumber's snake
Please God, please God
Please don't let him be another stumpy-humper, or a bush whacker
Please God not another plain-ole kill-joy-pussy-hater
Who jabs and pounds aimlessly, assaulting without mercy
Please God don't let him flounder and flap like a fish outta water

Holly shit!!!
He really does know what to do
He was not selfish either
And that tongue!!!
It sure could turn an atheist into a full fledge believer
The fella deserved his very own Zorro letter; F

Especially when he finally
God-dammit!
He laid those pipes!!!
Home-girl had forgotten she could sing opera
That was once you have the right director; someone who knew how
to work a stick!
Mr. So-and-So conducted the hell out of Miss Sandra Dee's organ
When it was over
She exhaled long, and oh so loud, in the back of that dark alley
Like a vampire coming down from a swoon

Possibilities/Step out of the box

She is back on the island after months of tragedy
Loss of a twenty year job, and the death of a beloved best friend
She is reevaluating her purpose in life
A broken relationship filled with mistrust
She has no children; she'd put it on the back burner
There were so many other things she had to accomplish
Now her spirit is broken
Chaotic mind, and hurting heart
She was on a rollercoaster of sporadic highs and crashing lows
Not knowing which way was up most days
Help
Please help a girl down she prayed

She looked out at azure blue waters
Blanketed by the snow white of chasing clouds that dotted a perfect
powder blue sky
That embraced the lush, verdant, landscape
A week had passed before she ventured out on the street among
people, feeling familiar eyes as they pierced her right through to the
heart
The sugary pearl-colored sand stung her feet from the glare of the
blazing sun's rays
Suddenly she felt the urge for something
Water would definitely not fulfill the need
Seeing as her clothing stuck to her as though she had bathed in a vat
of glue

She wandered aimlessly until she found that quaint shop
Inside she felt as though she had walked into a deep freeze, or a
forgotten part of heaven
She saw a boy; he smiled over at her licking on an ice cream
She had seen him before many times by the shop

She had even seen him up at the house, and riding on a bike pass her house
She had even seen him with the man behind the counter down at the beach

She waited her turn; last in line because she had strayed in search of something freezing to cool her raging body
Funny though, now she no longer felt she needed it
Because a cool breeze blew about her from every angle
It caressed her every being
It felt like she was being carried in the arms of calm
So much so that when her turn finally came
She settled on a container of sour-sop ice cream, with pineapple compote
She asked for the cone to be place on the top
"That's my boy's favorite." His voice pressed in on her thoughts.
"That's exactly how he liked it."
She offered nothing; she just gave him money and waited
"Coming out of the dark huh?" His mellow voice continued
She gave him a distracted smile, and lavished one on the boy standing not to far off in the corner licking on his cone.
"I put some cherries on top for a celebration of feeling once again. Trust me Miss."
"Thank you."
"You are welcome. "The name is Zion. Come see me again."

Couple days later she still couldn't seem to get the taste of the ice cream from her mouth
It troubled mind and body, and brought back memories she had long pushed aside, forbidding them to surface
She recalled a time of simple innocence; when she wouldn't hesitate to jump and fly by the seat of her pants, sucking on penny candies, and going about on bare feet
She scraped the bottom of the container praying that more would magically appear
However she refused to give in to the craving

124

She would make everything else work because she wasn't ready for all
the things that had cropped up
Mostly the hypnotic quality of his voice; that had reached way down
to the seat of her soul, and unlocked that rusty lock that kept her
from crumbling under its weight
She wouldn't have it
She couldn't have it
There was no time for any of it
Plus it hurt to damn much
But it seemed nothing was up to her anymore, everything was
conspiring

The sun's rays and the atmosphere reeked havoc
She refused to bend
She told herself she would not break
She couldn't help the smile that played about her face at the memory
of words from her mother
God bless her soul she thought, wherever she had gone to rest for an
eternity, or roam
"You de most stub'brunt and blindest once something get put in you
head."
The boy was back, as though taunting her; he had another ice cream
cone
"And you sure ain't get it from me. You get it from you father, that
ignorant mule. No wonder we couldn't set hass."
Laughter broke from within her and wandered out and beyond
It freed something from deep within

Someone or something had stolen the sun light
She looked up
"Miss…Daddy said to come give you this." He shoved a red sand
bucket at her
She reached out, and took the gift and looked inside
There was a tub of ice cream, with pineapple and cherries nestled
among crudely chipped ice
"He did, but why?" She asked
She looked at the boy no older than 7 or 8 years old

"Because he likes you silly. Why else?"

"He does?"

"Yes he does." The boy huffed.

He took a seat in front of her and licked hungrily at his ice cream cone

"But why?"

"Because it's about time you find a purpose. Eat…Go on eat." He coaxed

"This is so delicious. I can't remember tasting ice cream this, this…"

She couldn't find the words to describe the taste exploding around in her mouth

"Taste like how you want life to always be huh Miss Lilly?"

"How? How do you know my name?"

"I know many things, and mostly about you."

"You do? You are a most unusual boy. What is your name?"

"My name is Heart. Like the organ that beats in here." He said with a cocky smile, and touched his chest.

"Unusual."

"Indeed Miss Lilly, for a very unusual boy. Well so my daddy says. That was why they chose that name for me.

It was either her or me. It was a complicated birth. Such is life."

"You speak of things to adult Heart." She said looking at the beautiful child, as he sat before her, thinking that the only thing missing from him was wings.

"You have forgotten how to be. You have forgotten about living, and simply living once you were given many great things. You even forgot about taking time out for SELF

You have forgotten about how to enjoy a moment. You look but you don't see. Just think how excited my daddy was seeing you, and you didn't even notice. So many things are happening about you and you don't even notice. You don't even realize your Creator working in your life. Miss Lilly instead of dwelling on things you've lost, take stock of all you have accomplished, and will continue to. Nancy died not you. You promised her you would not allow her death to stop you from living. You promised that you would grieve and move on. But you can't move on unless you step out of the box. Come out of the

126

box Miss Lilly, come out and live again. My daddy is ready, and he is waiting."

He jumped to his feet and started walking away. "Life can be as sweet as that again, but only if you rise up and take a chance."

It took another couple of days before she trusted in the courage to walk back into the shop

He greeted her with the widest and warmest of smile, which caused her to shake like leaves to the whisper of passing wind

"Hello again Miss. Hope you enjoyed de ice cream?"

"I did. Thank you. Your boy is quite the talker. He gave me an earful. That is why I am here. I want to apologize for the other day."

"I don't understand." He said, a strange look coming to shroud his handsome face.

"Here is the bucket back." She handed it over to him

"Where did you get that?" He asked, and snatched the bucket from her hand.

"Your son Heart, spelt like the organ in here. He brought it to me with ice cream; that he claimed you sent to me."

"And when did that happen?"

"A couple of days ago."

"That could not be Miss." The man said in utter disbelief

"Call me Lilly. And why could that not be?" She mouthed with as much of the confusion as she saw crowding the man's face

"Because my son is dead! He died two years and two days ago to this date."

"But that can't be. Two days ago I sat with that boy!" She tossed, and pointed over at the photograph nestled on the top of the highest shelf. "He brought me sour sop ice cream with heaps of pineapple and cherries, in that red bucket, surrounded by chipped ice. He said it was a gift

from you. He was dressed in that same outfit, and he had an ice cream cone in his hand just like he is doing there."

I don't understand. He spoke to me as surely as I stand here speaking to you. And I have seen him with you many times walking the beach. I don't understand. I saw him! I saw that boy!" She said, as she gazed intently at the photograph.

He winked!

It winked over at her.

She slumped into a seat.

He couldn't stop himself. He walked to her.

He knew full well what and how she was feeling.

He too had seen him; first at the hospital when they had come to tell him he had finally died of the injuries he sustained when that car had knocked him off his bike.

Then at the church, and the burial ground.

Of course he hadn't said anything to anyone; who would say it was only his grief.

But he knew, and he believed.

He believed what she said she had seen.

He believed what he had seen.

He wrapped her in his arms.

She allowed him to hold her.

Until all she could manage with a tight voice was, "I am beginning to think out of the box. I am thinking out of the box."

In Dreams

She closed her eyes
She hadn't drift far
When she heard her name being called
She turned
You had no face
You held out a hand
She took it
Strange
She wasn't scared
She trusted you
Faceless and nameless
You pulled her close, and whispered in her ear
"You are the loveliest person I know."
You reined soft, sweet kisses on cheek and body
With confident hands you touched and touched
Blazing a lava trail that made her body sing with a strained rhapsody
and a sweet melodious delight
Of a rhythm familiar yet unattainable when awake
She is starved, so she begs, "Stay, please stay with me."
You said, "Wish I could."
As you steal away like wind in the willows
On breaths, only in dreams

What Do You Know For Sure?

That tomorrow's run behind yesterdays, like today for some
That once there is life there is hope
That not all who smile with you mean you well
That you can give, and give, and get nothing in return
That people will take you for granted
That you will be abused; physically, mentally, spiritually, emotionally, and financially
That trouble doesn't last always
You are up today, and could easily be down tomorrow
That love can creep up on you, scaring you to the core, making you act sillier than usual
That your son and daughter; children can peck and cut you until you bleed
That words hurt
That silence kills
That most of us are living from pay check to pay check; flying by the seat of our pants
That good sex can nourish, and bad can turn you into a mean spirited bitch
That friends can become lovers; that can turn into psycho-obsessed-anal-bastard's and bitches
That if you don't use proper hygiene you stink to high heaven
You just stink stink stink
That big-ass feet doesn't mean big dick
That small axe can cut big trees.
That big doesn't necessarily mean better
Especially when sex; in thought or deed pops up once or twice, as long as you are breathing
And girl! If not. You know someone who is out there having it as you are reading this
That words are words
That not all princes are charming
That sleeping doesn't make one beautiful

That love makes fools out of the best of us
That not all that glitters is gold
That not all clouds have silver linings or rainbows pots of gold
That not all who talk about sex is having it, or swinging from
chandeliers
That if you eat enough shit you will get fat, fat, fat
Weight sneaks on
That not everyone cheat
That you must always be aware
That Wacko-Jacko did not father kids the biblical way; insert penis
into vagina. And that 'sleep' in my bed means just that
That people will hurt you more times than not
That they will even kick you when you are down, and peck your flesh
clean from the bones today, and do it all again tomorrow
Care to add your own?

Injustice/ Man in Uniform

She hasn't seen Byron in days
It going on a week come this evening
But still she has to rise
She has to rise; get on with the rest of the day; the task at hand
She needs to persevere for their only child's sake
Meanwhile still trying to decipher how the man got pass all the road blocks
How on earth did he get between her legs?

The memory left a foul taste in the back of her throat Where booze-stained kisses lingered in her memory
It sullied her strong mind and sheets in a bout of rapturous and sweaty delight
So yes
She had trapped herself; she was now one of those statistics; a female running behind a baby-daddy; who was chasing everything in a skirt that passed in his path

Just think how it made her feel when Four-eyes took much pleasure in telling her what she saw
"I done seen your PC Byron and some female strolling arm in arm down at the bay front."
Lord have mercy
Lord have mercy
People she turned into someone people laughed at in plays, or in picture shows
She skulked in bushes, jumped over high walls, and little ones too
She even ran alongside moving vehicles, straining her neck and eyes to catch a glimpse of the new-chick-on-the-block
Having long since lost faith in the lyrics; don't ask my neighbor, that he so loved to sing
"See that is de kind of shit that breaks up a happy home, and bring strive in decent relationships. So why fix it if it ain't broke." He used to say

Man! Was she dumb or what
Don't forget that while he was saying all that shit he was getting his
every need met
She was cooking gourmet island meals, displayed on lavish layouts,
washing and ironing; putting straight as his Pinocchio-shaped-half-
breed nose to his uniform and clothing
She made him the envy of many as he strutted about like a conceited
peacock
He acted as though he was running some popularity contest
Better yet like the President of the island
As though he had a license to rape and plot murder
To plunder and pillage all while he wore a uniform; carte blanch to
perpetrate one's carnal desires and lasciviousness
Having everything and everyone at his beck and call

"Well I am only telling you what Two-tongue and myself done seen
with these-here eyes."
She stood there stupidly looking deep within these-here eyes,
wondering which pair she had seen PC Byron with
But that wasn't what was really important in the long run
Seeing as she had become her very own Private investigator

Lord!
You should have seen this woman PC Byron keeping company with
Immediately she promised to stop beating up on herself
Because the woman looked like a starving nanny-goat
She couldn't believe how that lying-lazy-lizard-like bastard
PC Byron was lovingly gazing into her bug eyes
Not to forget that ass of hers, and those hips; wider than an American
highway, and belly; high as a coal pit mound
She had to stop herself short of running across a traffic filled street
when they stopped off at Mike's Bar
For under the glaring street light the sistah looked like Jack Sprat's
wife
But you should see the attentive way PC Byron was being to the
Raggedy Ann

She was transported back to the house
Where she would ask him to help her out; by passing her something
PC Byron would bark and snarl like a nasty alley dog
As though they were on different continents
One time she had said to him, "Let's go for a walk."
She wanted to create some so-call-intimacy
"I am tired." He barked.
"Cuddle me PC Byron."
"You not a baby Justice."
"Dinner and a movie then?"
"Thank you. I'll have it right here in front of the television."
It continued like that for up to three years
She had put up with a walking-sleeping-dead
Who huffed and puffed, pulled and tugged, pushed and pumped
So many times she had wanted to fall asleep while he slobbered and
floundered about between her legs
He had managed to impregnate her, and how in the hell that
happened was beyond her
It just goes to show; lie down with dogs and you get up with fleas
"A female has to do her best. Men are a scarce commodity, especially
good-God-fearing ones with decent jobs."
That according to the Gospel of Island Mothers
So you must do to the best of your/black female's ability
You are groomed for slavery from the time you are forced out of
safety; between the most sacred of flesh that is taken for granted
Females can't figure out 'its' worth, and men just can't get enough,
they use it like we breathe the air
So the pattern continues, and mama tells you, "You cannot be
anything without a man at your side."
Never mind how she wait on daddy; God bless his wretched-lazy-ass
The way she waited on that man hand and foot with never a please or
thank you out of his mouth
That no doubt was the cause of her going to an early grave
But let her or her brother Manual; the lady at the register office
placed an A at the end where there should have been an E
Anyway islanders eat most letters because of the dialect

This should not be an excuse, but at times some things just are for the sake of survival
They had to find a way to cope; make it through the racial battlefield of distinction and division
But back to Manny; who forgot the magic words one day and war broke out at house number 10 in Cherry Street
Mama turned into a professional sport associate; throwing missiles, dodging, jumping, and sprinting
Guess enlightenment dawned for him, but more so for her

She thought and thought and thought some more about what had drove her into PC Byron's treacherous tentacles
Could it be the fact that most thought she was an old-maid at 25?
Or better yet that she played patter-cake with her coochie?
Truth though; she had vowed to never be anything like her mama; being at a man's beck and call because she was dick-whipped, or afraid to be on her own
She wanted to make her own way; she ran a boarding house
That no doubt impressed PC Byron when he set foot inside
He even paid up three months in advance
He said, "I have every faith in you Lady Justice."
He smiled that Mr. Clean gleam-in-teeth smile, with eyes that never left hers
They glistened with what she thought was pride
She fell for it hook, line and sinker
Building an entire castle on a foundation of sand
While he played her like a Stradivarius violin
He brought her a sprig some flower, and sat and listened while she went on about all her future plans
She thought how intently he was listened to her
Only now she reckoned he was only plotting so intensely
Months later after a chanced encounter; where he played her starving being like a concert piano
She was tired of the last one; Rafael; the two-timer who didn't like ambitious females
He thought they were trifling
Especially when his good seed could never take no root

Rafael called her a cold hearted and spiteful bitch, and shouted for
the world to hear that her stomach was a grave yard
Yes
So how in the hell did PC Byron get in and so far to almost strip her
of everything?
She became many things, and yet nothing to that tall-creamy-
smoother- than-melting-ice cream-running-down-a-cone conman
She became his mama, banker, creditor, debt consolidator, parole
officer, punching bag, doormat, priest, and mattress
Plain and simply put; she just became his bitch

She reached for the pot of rice and peas, her muscles seized and the
pot went crashing to the floor
All eyes flew to the mess
Images of her life flashed through her mind's eye
As she continued she saw judgment in all eyes
It reined down
She thought of a phrase; who don't know you, call you YOU
Mercy knew that here mama was not the same
Anyone could see her mama was not as vibrant as she once was
She forgets things, and seemed to spend most times crying
Many times she would come upon her; lost in thought and staring at
hands; misshapen and swollen
For PC Byron had beaten her within an inch of her life one night
with his Billy-club
Mercy was to little to protect her mama from the vigorous blows
of that that contradictory stick; such beauty and craftsmanship; in
genius length and pliable gloss
Mercy recalled how PC Byron pushed her forcibly when she ran in the
way to protect her mama's body; that ended up covering her instead
It resulted in a slew of cutting kicks
Mercy thought at the time that perhaps his hands had gotten tired
"Why are you hurting my mama?" Mercy asked
"Because she is nothing but a trick; a whore." He tossed.
With that said, he spat on her over and again
Then he turned his nastiness to the surrounding; breaking almost
everything before he stumbled off into the night

Mercy thought, what do I do? Who do I turn to?
All her screams had brought no one, as her mama's body lay lifeless
Mercy had begged her to open her eyes, but she didn't
Mercy reckoned she didn't, not because she didn't but because she just simply couldn't
For how long she had laid there with her mama's lifeless body she had lost track
That is until she felt her stir; as though the creatures who lived in the floor boards had breathed life back into her
Then the neighbors started tumbling out and mumbling
Her grandfather and the man she had known as a beloved father and daddy; who had pulverized her mama were talking
Mercy turned away from them, she hated them both, and vowed she would hate them for as long as she lived
Perhaps all male at that precise moment
Especially when her grandfather told her to hush-up, that the man in uniform was right to hit her mama, because she should have come straight home after she was finished with work.
Dead silence as Mercy looked from him to the man
Dead silence now as Mercy looked from her mama to the mess on the floor, and back to her mama again
Please don't let her see the feelings; accusation and blame
Please dear God don't let her see negativity
Too late!
Instantly her mama spun on her heels and hobbled off
Had she seen them; these feelings registered in her eyes
For they do crop up occasionally
"I am sorry baby, I am so very sorry. I didn't mean to embarrass you."
Her mama said.
Mercy's legs felt as though they were fitted with cement blocks as she tried to get to the woman

When Mercy got to her mama; the woman was in a heap outside the front door
No doubt flashes of that night danced about in her head
It flashed in her mind's eye

Mercy rushed to her mama, "we can eat something else. It is just food. All can be replaced."

"But what can replace these?" Her mama asked, as she held up hands; that had never mended. "Think I don't see the way you always hover when I reach for him." She offered, nodding over at her grandson

"I am so sorry mama. I didn't mean to seem as if I don't trust." Mercy said.

"And so you shouldn't. It is so hard out there. Especially the things we say and do/in our actions towards each other under the guise of love. For how can we claim love when we can't even care; love in its simplest measure." Her mama asked.

Mercy couldn't answer, she had nothing to offer

The afternoon was stagnant and balmy

It was the sort of afternoon that made clothes feel like barnacles about your neck, and armor to the body

Where shoes hang like weights, and food felt like sharp punches in the gut

So everyone decided the only place to be was at the beach

It was Granny Justice's birthday, and she felt old ancient and decrepit, every time she looked at her hands

The severity had not gone unnoticed, even though she had been hiding them for years

However today the oppressive heat and humidity was everyone's arch rival

Even her mama Justice who had no choice but to leave the hands above board like evidence to a judge in the courtroom

"Tell me about them." Her grandson urged.

"Tell you what?" She asked, as she pulled her hands from his. "Tell you about man's injustice to man? Tell you about the injustice that parade about the island in uniform?

"Yes Granny tell me."

"Well let me ask you this. If a tree falls in the forest does it not make a sound?"

"Yes granny. Tell me. I am listening."

"Then I will tell you about the girl who once believed in happily ever after, and prince charming, and pots of gold with rainbows at the end. That happiness was there for all to grab if you reached out.

That when you give respect you got it back, and if you worked hard
and saved you can build castles
But it seemed as though I missed out on class the day they taught
the lesson on protecting oneself from wolves who parade in sheep
clothing."
A sort of laughter escaped her
It sent chills through the bones, and fright to mind
"Be aware child. For 'they' will come a knocking as surely as I sit here
with you and these feeble hands; that are failing day after day.
Believe me when I say to you never doubt when a person shows you
upfront who they are. If it walks like a duck and quacks like one,
believe that it is a duck.
Sweet boy, sheep never bring goat, and neither does the apple fall far
from the tree.
What good for goose is not necessarily good for gander. Child those
figure heads will not always protect you. Especially if the perpetrator
is one of their own
But you asked about my hands right?"
"Yes granny."
"Well my hands are like this because I finally learned that I could
do bad all by myself. I dared believe I could do better. I no longer
wanted to be held back.
It didn't feel right, and I no longer desired to stay silent.
I wanted to finally break the chains, make my own mark in this
world, and create my own truth. I found wings, and I wanted to soar;
high, fly free.
I said no more, I had had enough. I shouted too hard when I found
my voice.
He tried to silence me, and child no one lifted a finger to help.
No one; not queen, and certainly not country.
He was protected like so many others who wore uniforms to disguise
the real monsters they are
Monsters that are thriving daily
But I am learning
Granny is learning
To release negative patterns; those that were handed down through
generations."

Aftermath

Is it crazy to think you can still smell him everywhere?
On your clothes, skin, lips, and deep between your legs
Not to forget among your pillows and sheet
Embedded in your carpet and oozing from your walls
Reach out
Touch it
Just like he touched you all night long, even into the wee hours of the morning
He has marked you like an animal his territory
Yet you don't seem to mind
Not even if it turns out that he played you?
No you say
Want to know why

Well for years she used to think that there was something seriously wrong
Why the touch of a man just left her feeling cold
To the point she reckoned why bother
Why waste the precious breath the Creator gave?
For some things are just so, and others are simply meant to be left alone
But he has come along now to prove her wrong
For it is days after and she still craved him; friend and lover
Who makes her think that anything is possible
She is composing; writing odes of every suckle and delicious bite, every kind word
Her trust is refueled and renewed
She is enlightened, curious, and hungry to the point of depression
Humbled that she had to eat her words
That there was none who understood her need
Oh these creatures God created
How they confused her
She doesn't know why, understand why

Yet she is yearning and wanting
Yearning for her dark chocolate brother
Who listened and who actually cared that she got off
Just as much, or even before he did

Black Eye Peas

They look like eyes staring back at me granny
Angry eyes
Sad eyes
Mischievous and vex eyes
Scolding and blaming eyes
Wandering and roaming
They watch when I move here and there
If I look away and back again there they are
I don't want them
 I don't like them
Seems like everywhere I go there they are
Stop sharing them granny
Stop growing them
Stop cooking them
And no more decorating the freezer with them
They are no good for anything
Just staring, staring, staring
I don't want them
I don't like them
That is until the day my brother Johnny's elbow backed up into my lip
Oh sweet mystery at last I found thee!
Such comforting relief when granny slapped a bag straight from the
freezer against them
Black eye peas became a friend, and later a trusting confidant
Especially when Lenny the ex husband gave me my first shiner
That I tried to hide from friends and family; granny especially
Because I never doubted she would have cooked up a batch of my
enemies turned ally
For those angry and sad eyes
Mischievous and vex eyes
Scolding and blaming eyes
Were the last he would have seen as he wandered off to sweet glory
For my friends would have been resting maliciously in his trifling gut

Yearning

Eyes stinging
Heart yearning
Crotch weeping; wet hungry
Longing for a taste of you
The way you would stroke the soft fleshy folds
Making them beg in anticipation
Sing in a sultry Billie Holiday crescendo of melodious rhapsody
To that slow lingering torture-some beat
That makes one howl in fits of surprise
Yes!
Yes!
Oh God yes!!!
You actually knew where to put tongue and fingers
Seeking every crack and groove
Frenzy
Oh yes!
 Oh God yes!
You are feeling in places only imagined
Now they are hot and searing, heady and pungent
As you plunged deep within, touching the pussy's soul
You are transported to heaven on wings of wantonness
You pray to God let me die, please let me die in this bed of heat and
desire
On sheets of sweat and blood stain wrinkles, heady with juices of
commingled madness
Then your organ departs
It is still throbbing inside
While lies and deceit scamper about haunting like the Grim Reaper
Staleness lingers, as aloofness trudges and tramples in
Tying your limbs
No tender touches anymore
No spewing of kind words
No calls on the days rolling in

So you become a woman tainted, with time as her confidant
You have soiled body, heart, mind, and the pussy's soul
So much so that at the touch of another she cringes
Imagining your hand where they used to burn trails of fire
Etching pleasure like lava tracks
She made a vow; I will give my crotch the pleasure it seeks
The satisfaction it craves like needles full of something, anything to a junkie
Down to the organ it needs, opening wide
And yes!
Yes!
Yes!
She will holler to the rafters
To moon and stars, and sun and clouds
She will let them take pleasure
She will open wide, wide, wider
Only now the lesson is learned
She is smarter
She thinks and she doesn't forget
That simply put; a fucker fucks, and a fuck is just that

Mr. B

Alone
In mind, body, and the soul
They are all yearning
So she thought to turn on the television
However she couldn't remember where the remote was
Seeing Jay would be the first and the last to handle the blasted thing
And by handling she meant just that
The thing is like an appendage
He no longer sees it fit to talk anymore
Not even to see or listen
As he flicks uncaring of anything else through the channels
Sports; cricket basketball baseball tennis...
The fool even sits through darts and poker

One day you should have heard the way he shouted at her
It would have even come to blows if the damn thing hadn't popped
up from under the cushion
Probably the Fate's were trying to tell or show him them something
So he would take notice of that tight number she had poured her
tormented frame into
Just so she wouldn't go stark raving mad from being ignored
Or worst yet hand herself over pitifully to the toy-boy down at the
supermarket
Who noticed everything different about her
"Nice do, pretty shade of lipstick, hot shoes, killer legs"
"Hope your Mister appreciates what he has?"
"No he doesn't!" She thought
He doesn't even know she exists anymore!"
Contempt longed to scream
She wanted to plead with him, "take me right there and then. Here
on the check out line."
But all she managed was, "thank you."
Thinking he sure would make some girl or boy happy one day

Only hope she or he appreciated him
But as much attention as she got
She only had eyes for Jay; who only had eyes for his one-eyed beast
Who was always there in her goddam-face
Looking and laughing
Stealing her husband's attention and affection
No appreciation for anything she cooked up to entice him and make
herself a little happy in the process
"Didn't you pay the electricity bill?" He asked her
One day when he came upon her bathed in candle light and draped
across his throne
Yes you fat-lazy-pig, she thought, but she struck a most provocative
pose instead
 "Can't you see what I did for you?" She teased.
"Oh snap! You mean?"
He turned his back, "Baby please just let me catch my breath and I
promise I will be all yours."
Then he reached over her to grab for the remote
He caressed it giving it more play than he gives to her throbbing
bulging starving clit
When he got the rare urges
Like when she conveniently forgets to pay
the cable bill

Leaves

Leaves blown
Tossed high
Blown here
Blown there
Blown everywhere
They are frustrated, unkind, unfeeling, and uncaring
They are starved of affection and feeling
Fly leaves
Fly high
Fly with our hopes
Fly with our dreams
Fly with our future
Troubled, and so filled with despair

About the Author;

Kathleen is a daughter of Montserrat; land of a multicultural, diverse, and artistic people.

She has always aspired to be a writer, loving to weave words together and watch and listen to see the stories they tell, whether by reading, writing, or singing.

She has learned over the years that words play an important part in shaping who she has become today.

Harsh and critical words as a youth use too send her in hiding; retreating into self, as much as they made her cry. Just like kind words.

Inside herself she learned uplifting and congratulatory, inspiring and conquering words, that now has her walking out and taking center stage; owning and showing.

She only wants to tell others to believe in themselves. Take it, show it, own it, be it.

Stay tuned, for there are still so much more to come.

Thank you to all who has touched her life and made a difference.

From an eye contact, to a word; any word.

Thank you mama, daddy, mom, and George, sisters, brothers, cousins, nieces, nephews, aunts, uncles, and friends; old and new; from America and now here in the UK. You know who you are. I will love you 'all' always.

14605784R00097

Printed in Great Britain
by Amazon.co.uk, Ltd.,
Marston Gate.